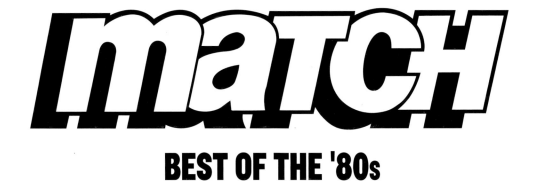

BEST OF THE '80s

BOXTREE

First published 2008 by Boxtree
an imprint of Pan Macmillan Ltd
Pan Macmillan,
20 New Wharf Road,
London N1 9RR
Basingstoke and Oxford
Associated companies throughout the world
www.panmacmillan.com

Editor: Tim Street
Art Director: Darryl Tooth
Production Editor: Oli Reed
Sub-Editor: Darren Cross
Writer/Sub-Editor: Tim Unwin
Thanks to: Kevin Keegan and Sue Battey at
Newcastle United FC, Nikki Palmer, Phil Bagnall,
Mel Bagnall, Graham Lampard at Craftsman
Binders, Lara Thorns and Jim Brown at Coventry
City FC, Martin Ellis at PA Photos, Billy Robertso
at Action Images, Andreas Nilsson at the
Swedish FA and the rest of the MATCH team.

ISBN 978-0-7522-2676-7

A CIP catalogue record for this book is available
from the British Library.

Colour Origination by Gildenburgh Ltd
Printed by Printer Trento

Visit www.panmacmillan.com to read more
about all our books and to buy them. You will
also find features, author interviews and news
of any author events, and you can sign up for
e-newsletters so that you're always first
to hear about our new releases.

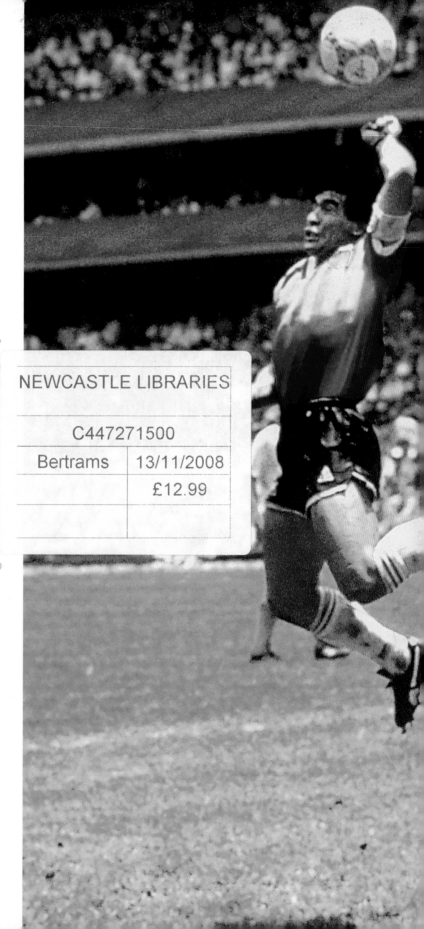

CONTENTS

FOREWORD
BY KEVIN KEEGAN, OBE

I signed for MATCH Weekly on September 6, 1979 – the magazine's launch issue. For 25p, you could win a trip to the European Championship Finals in Italy.

I was the first cover star of MATCH, joining regular columnists Steve Coppell, Jimmy Hill and Ossie Ardiles. In my first issue, I taught readers how to be a great striker in 'Learn To Play The Keegan Way'.

This book looks back at the events, stars, beards and mullets of the 1980s. The dominance of Liverpool, the arrival of Gazza, Rush, Lineker, The Hand of God, Captain Marvel, Wimbledon, Bradford, Heysel and Hillsborough. We said a sad farewell to Bill Shankly, but other great managers were plying their trade – Paisley, Clough, Robson, Ferguson and Venables to name just a few.

I hope this book brings back a few memories for you.

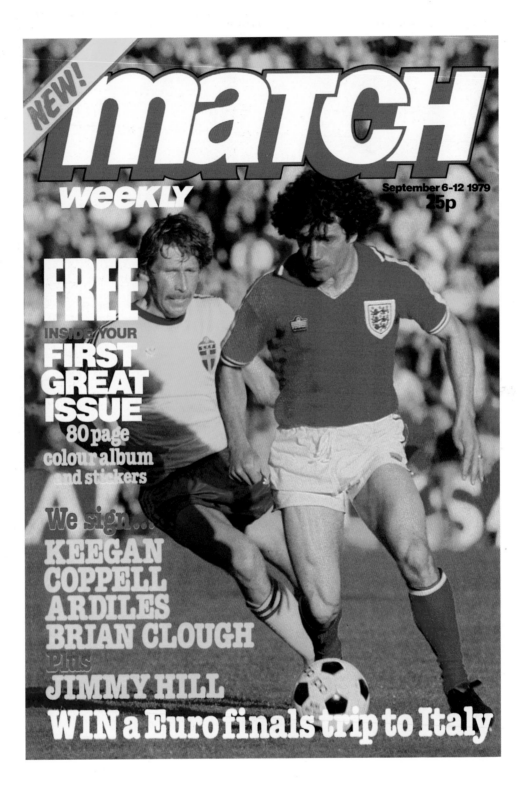

NEW!

MATCH

weekly

September 6-12 1979
25p

FREE
INSIDE YOUR
**FIRST
GREAT
ISSUE**
80 page
colour album
and stickers

We sign...
**KEEGAN
COPPELL
ARDILES
BRIAN CLOUGH**
Plus
JIMMY HILL
WIN a Euro finals trip to Italy

1979-80

A £1 million teenager,
two Wembley upsets
and a brown kit.

1979-80

Terry McDermott

FIRST ISSUE!

September 6, 1979

Kevin Keegan becomes the first ever cover star of MATCH Weekly, seen here playing for England against Sweden's Conny Torstensson the previous June, a friendly that ended 0-0. Issue one comes with an 80-page sticker album.

KING OSSIE!

March 8, 1980

Spurs midfielder Ossie Ardiles pips Trevor Francis to win £100 and the title of the first MATCHMAN Of The Month. The award, based on a player's match rating, continues to this day, though now without the financial reward.

LEAGUE CUP FINAL!

March 22, 1980

Andy Gray's strike beats an all-star Nottingham Forest side. Reacting to Wolves assistant Richie Barker's claim that Forest can still win the European Cup, Brian Clough says: "At the moment, I couldn't lift a glass of champagne."

FA CUP SPECIAL!

May 10, 1980

Arsenal beat Liverpool in the semi-finals after 420 minutes and three replays. Kevin Keegan predicts a 'five-goal thriller' in the final, while West Ham star Billy Bonds says he'll have a swig of whisky in the dressing room 'for luck'.

HAPPY HAMMERS!

May 17, 1980

West Ham become the last team from outside the top flight to lift the FA Cup. Trevor Brooking scores with a rare header by turning in what Stuart Pearson later admitted was a shot. Paul Allen appears in the final at just 17 years and 256 days.

Glenn Hoddle

>> STAR PLAYERS!

TERRY McDERMOTT, Liverpool:
The all-action midfielder's accurate passing and hard running helped The Reds win their fifth league title in eight seasons. Macca netted an impressive 14 goals and earned an England squad place for the 1980 European Championships in Italy.

GLENN HODDLE, Tottenham:
The classy young midfielder enjoyed a fantastic season for Spurs and England. He scored 19 league goals and netted on his England debut against Bulgaria, showing the sort of grace and skill that hadn't been seen in the English game for many years.

BEST KIT!
England's Admiral home kit.

WORST KIT!
Coventry's brown away kit.

>> SEASON HIGHLIGHTS!

JULY: Nottingham Forest pay a club record £500,000 for Leeds left-back Frank Gray.

AUGUST: Liverpool beat Arsenal 3-1 in the Charity Shield season warm-up at Wembley.

SEPTEMBER: Man. City break the British transfer record by paying £1.45 million for midfielder Steve Daley. Wolves replace Daley with Aston Villa's Andy Gray for a similar fee.

OCTOBER: England's 1966 World Cup hero Geoff Hurst is named as the new manager of Division Two Chelsea.

NOVEMBER: England striker Tony Woodcock makes a shock move from Nottingham Forest to German giants Cologne.

DECEMBER: The FA sign a four-year television deal thought to be worth £6 million.

JANUARY: Non-league Harlow knock Division Two high-flyers Leicester out of the FA Cup.

FEBRUARY: European Player Of The Year Kevin Keegan agrees a summer move to Southampton from Hamburg.

MARCH: Wolves beat Nottingham Forest 1-0 in the League Cup final.

APRIL: Liverpool pay £300,000 for Chester's 18-year-old striker Ian Rush – a record fee for Chester to this day.

MAY: Nottingham Forest retain the European Cup in Madrid, beating Bayern Munich 1-0.

JUNE: West Germany win Euro '80 - Horst Hrubesch nets both goals as they beat Belgium 2-1.

Pele, Bobby Moore, Ardiles and Beattie are among the players who star in a new war film

Just champion, dad!

Andy Gray
Wolves
and Scotland

Clockwise from top: Filming starts on Escape To Victory, Andy Gray moves to Wolves for £1.4 million, Kevin Keegan returns to England after two seasons with Hamburg, Kenny and Paul Dalglish celebrate The Reds' title after a 4-1 win against Aston Villa.

KEEGAN: What the Saints say

>> RISING STARS!

ALEX FERGUSON: For the first time since 1965, a team from outside Glasgow were crowned Scottish champions. Fergie's Aberdeen, which included Willie Miller, Gordon Strachan, Alex McLeish and Steve Archibald, beat Celtic by one point.

CLIVE ALLEN: After hitting 28 goals for QPR, the 19-year-old striker became Britain's first £1 million teenager. Arsenal boss Terry Neill said it would be a 'happy marriage', but Allen made no competitive appearances for The Gunners and joined Crystal Palace two months later.

>> FINAL LEAGUE TABLES!

DIVISION ONE

	CLUB	P	W	D	L	F	A	GD	Pts
1	Liverpool	42	25	10	7	81	30	+51	60
2	Man. United	42	24	10	8	65	35	+30	58
3	Ipswich	42	22	9	11	68	39	+29	53
4	Arsenal	42	18	16	8	52	36	+16	52
5	Nott'm Forest	42	20	8	14	63	43	+20	48
6	Wolves	42	19	9	14	58	47	+11	47
7	Aston Villa	42	16	14	12	51	50	+1	46
8	Southampton	42	18	9	15	65	53	+12	45
9	Middlesbrough	42	16	12	14	50	44	+6	44
10	West Brom	42	11	19	12	54	50	+4	41
11	Leeds	42	13	14	15	46	50	-4	40
12	Norwich	42	13	14	15	58	66	-8	40
13	Crystal Palace	42	12	16	14	41	50	-9	40
14	Tottenham	42	15	10	17	52	62	-10	40
15	Coventry	42	16	7	19	56	66	-10	39
16	Brighton	42	11	15	16	47	57	-10	37
17	Man. City	42	12	13	17	43	66	-23	37
18	Stoke	42	13	10	19	44	58	-14	36
19	Everton	42	9	17	16	43	51	-8	35
20	Bristol City	42	9	13	20	37	66	-29	31
21	Derby	42	11	8	23	47	67	-20	30
22	Bolton	42	5	15	22	38	73	-35	25

TOP SCORER: *Phil Boyer Southampton, 23 goals*

DIVISION TWO

	CLUB	P	W	D	L	F	A	GD	Pts
1	Leicester	42	21	13	8	58	38	+20	55
2	Sunderland	42	21	12	9	69	42	+27	54
3	Birmingham	42	21	11	10	58	38	+20	53
4	Chelsea	42	23	7	12	66	52	+14	53
5	QPR	42	18	13	11	75	53	+22	49
6	Luton	42	16	17	9	66	45	+21	49
7	West Ham	42	20	7	15	54	43	+11	47
8	Cambridge	42	14	16	12	61	53	+8	44
9	Newcastle	42	15	14	13	53	49	+4	44
10	Preston	42	12	19	11	56	52	+4	43
11	Oldham	42	16	11	15	49	53	-4	43
12	Swansea	42	17	9	16	48	53	-5	43
13	Shrewsbury	42	18	5	19	60	53	+7	41
14	Orient	42	12	17	13	48	54	-6	41
15	Cardiff	42	16	8	18	41	48	-7	40
16	Wrexham	42	16	6	20	40	49	-9	38
17	Notts County	42	11	15	16	51	52	-1	37
18	Watford	42	12	13	17	39	46	-7	37
19	Bristol Rovers	42	11	13	18	50	64	-14	35
20	Fulham	42	11	7	24	42	74	-32	29
21	Burnley	42	6	15	21	39	73	-34	27
22	Charlton	42	6	15	21	39	78	-39	22

TOP SCORER: *Clive Allen QPR, 28 goals*

DIVISION THREE

	CLUB	P	W	D	L	F	A	GD	Pts
1	Grimsby	46	26	10	10	73	42	+31	62
2	Blackburn	46	25	9	12	58	36	+22	59
3	Sheff. Wed.	46	21	16	9	81	47	+34	58
4	Chesterfield	46	23	11	12	71	46	+25	57
5	Colchester	46	20	12	14	64	56	+8	52
6	Carlisle	46	18	12	16	66	56	+10	48
7	Reading	46	16	16	14	66	65	+1	48
8	Exeter	46	19	10	17	60	68	-8	48
9	Chester	46	17	13	16	49	57	-8	47
10	Swindon	46	19	8	19	71	63	+8	46
11	Barnsley	46	16	14	16	53	56	-3	46
12	Sheff. United	46	18	10	18	60	66	-6	46
13	Rotherham	46	18	10	18	58	66	-8	46
14	Millwall	46	16	13	17	65	59	+6	45
15	Plymouth	46	16	12	18	59	55	+4	44
16	Gillingham	46	14	14	18	49	51	-2	42
17	Oxford	46	14	13	19	57	62	-5	41
18	Blackpool	46	15	11	20	62	74	-12	41
19	Brentford	46	15	11	20	59	73	-14	41
20	Hull	46	12	16	18	51	69	-18	40
21	Bury	46	16	7	23	45	59	-14	39
22	Southend	46	14	10	22	47	58	-11	38
23	Mansfield	46	10	16	20	47	58	-11	36
24	Wimbledon	46	10	14	22	52	81	-29	34

TOP SCORER: *Terry Curran Sheffield Wednesday, 22 goals*

DIVISION FOUR

	CLUB	P	W	D	L	F	A	GD	Pts
1	Huddersfield	46	27	12	7	101	48	+53	66
2	Walsall	46	23	18	5	75	47	+28	64
3	Newport	46	27	7	12	83	50	+33	61
4	Portsmouth	46	24	12	10	91	49	+42	60
5	Bradford	46	24	12	10	77	50	+27	60
6	Wigan	46	21	13	12	76	61	+15	55
7	Lincoln	46	18	17	11	64	42	+22	53
8	Peterborough	46	21	10	15	58	47	+11	52
9	Torquay	46	15	17	14	70	69	+1	47
10	Aldershot	46	16	13	17	62	53	+9	45
11	Bournemouth	46	13	18	15	52	51	+1	44
12	Doncaster	46	15	14	17	62	63	-1	44
13	Northampton	46	16	12	18	51	66	-15	44
14	Scunthorpe	46	14	15	17	58	75	-17	43
15	Tranmere	46	14	13	19	50	56	-6	41
16	Stockport	46	14	12	20	48	72	-24	40
17	York	46	14	11	21	65	82	-17	39
18	Halifax	46	13	13	20	46	72	-26	39
19	Hartlepool	46	14	10	22	59	64	-5	38
20	Port Vale	46	12	12	22	56	70	-14	36
21	Hereford	46	11	14	21	38	52	-14	36
22	Darlington	46	9	17	20	50	74	-24	35
23	Crewe	46	11	13	22	35	68	-33	35
24	Rochdale	46	7	13	26	33	79	-46	27

TOP SCORER: *Colin Garwood Aldershot, 27 goals (17 for Portsmouth)*

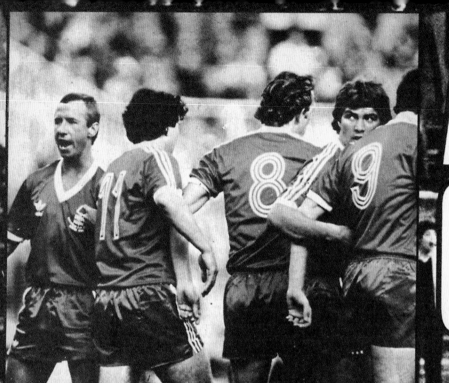

ACE
CLU

FORES

**Action highlights
from a glory
night in Madrid**

EURO KINGS

IN PICTURE: Forest skipper John
[Mc]Govern (4) embraces John Robertson
[aft]er he'd scored the 20th minute
[ma]tch-winner in Madrid as Ian Bowyer (8)
[an]d Larry Lloyd (5) join the celebrations.

[TO]P LEFT: Typical of Forest's victory . . . a
[...] wall that holds Hamburg at bay. Here
[Joh]n McGovern organises his defence of,
[fro]m the left, Robertson, Bowyer, Mills and
[...]tles.

BOTTOM LEFT: Forest hero Peter Shilton,
foils Kevin Keegan's flying dive.

TOP RIGHT: We are the champions!
Dressing room hi-jinks as Forest celebrate
with the Cup. Back row (left to right): Bryn
Gunn, Dave Needham, Viv Anderson. Middle
row: Martin O'Neil, John Robertson, Jim
Montgomery, Peter Shilton, Ian Bowyer,
Larry Lloyd, Garry Birtles, John O'Hare,

Kenny Burns and Frank Gray. Front: John
McGovern and assistant manager Peter
Taylor.

EUROPEAN CUP FINAL

NOTTINGHAM FOREST (1) 1 (Robertson 20)
HAMBURG (W. Germany) (0) 0
Att: 75,000 (in Madrid)
Forest: Shilton 9, Anderson 7, Gray 7 (Gunn),
McGovern 8, Lloyd 8, *BURNS 10, O'Neil 8, Bowyer
8, Birtles 9, Mills 7 (O'Hare 7), Robertson 8.
Hamburg: Kargus 6, Kaltz 7, Nogly 8, Jakobs 7,
Buljan 7, Hieronymus 6 (Hrubesch 7), Keegan 7,
Memering 7, Mileski 7, *MAGATH 8, Reimann 6.
Referee: Mr A. Garrido (Portugal).
MATCH RATING: ****

TALBOT TURNS 3 ACES ♣ 4

BRADY HAS BETTER LEGS THAN BRITT

I CO'LEARY RE MOVES FASTER & THAN A F BRITISH RAIL R N L

TALBOT STRIKES BETTER THAN LEYLAND

RIX SELLS MORE DUMMIES THAN MOTHERCARE

Match Weekly produces better pictures than Metro Goldwyn Mayer . . . no Cup Final would be complete without the special brand of football humour captured here on the banners of the Arsenal fans. But it was West Ham who had the last laugh.

This was the very last moment of action from the 1980 Cup Final. The ref is blowing for time and Hammer Paul Allen is already on his knees. But Arsenal's Willie Young (6) is still challenging for the ball with Ray Stewart.

It's all over for Arsenal. The expre on the faces of Liam Brady (nearest camera), Alan Sunderland (arm rais and Sammy Nelson say it all.

'Our great

Man of the Match Trevor Brooking in elegant action during the Final as he tussles with Arsenal's Talbot.

Let's celebrate. Trevor Brooking, fist clenched in salute, gets a hug that says well done from skipper Billy Bonds (4). They are about to be joined by Alvin Martin. And just look at that victory leap from West Ham's Ray Stewart (far right).

Below: *The moment of truth for Arsenal's Pat Rice (left) and Brian Talbot as Hammers' midfield man Alan Devonshire gets round the back to supply the cross which finally led to West Ham's winner.*

Pictures: DUNCAN CUBITT

st moment' – JOHN LYALL

Best day in club's history says West Ham boss

THE GOALS THAT GOT AWAY....

IF EVER a team were near and yet so far from glory then it was England in their crunch European Championship clash against Italy.

It's history now that it was Italy's Tardelli who scored the only goal of the game just 10 minutes from the end. But it could have been so different.

Twice England crashed the ball against the Italian woodwork, and after linking neatly with Ray Kennedy, Kevin Keegan had a left foot effort superbly saved by 'keeper Dino Zoff.

MATCH WEEKLY photographer Duncan Cubitt was in the packed Stadio Communale in Turin to capture the goals that got away.

Left: Ray Kennedy lashes a superb volley past the outstretched leg of Gentile only to see it smack against Dino Zoff's left hand post. Looking on is Graziani (20).

Below left: It's chaos in the Italian penalty area as a cross from England's right flank falls to Sansom on the far post. Zoff fails to reach the England full-back's right foot shot but again the ball canons off a post. Pictured left to right are: Steve Coppell, Bettega, Benetti, Collovati, Tardelli, Zoff and Sansom.

Below: Kevin Keegan can't believe it as Zoff gets down well to claw his left foot shot past the post. Ray Kennedy, who laid on the chance, looks on expectantly.

Europa 80

EUROPEAN CHAMPIONSHIPS

MATCH MAKERS

ARNOLD MUHREN
Ipswich and Holland

FULL NAME: Arnoldus Johannes Hyacintus Muhren
BIRTHPLACE/DATE: Volendam, Holland. June 2, 1951.
HEIGHT/WEIGHT: 5ft 11in, 10½st.
MARRIED: Yes, to Jeerie
CHILDREN: Arjan (4), Claudia (2)
CAR: Chrysler Talbot.
PREVIOUS CLUBS: Volendam, Ajax, Twente Enschede (all Holland).
TRADE BEFORE TURNING PRO: Office boy in my Uncle's furniture firm.
CLUB NICKNAME: 'Arnie'
WORST EVER INJURY: Calf muscle strain.
FAVOURITE FOOTBALL LEAGUE PLAYER: Frans Thijssen, my Ipswich pal. He is such a good dribbler and defender. He's also difficult to dispossess.
FAVOURITE OTHER TEAM: Liverpool.
FAVOURITE FOREIGN PLAYER AND WHY: Johan Cruyff. He has everything, so quick and skilful.
BEST ALL TIME BRITISH TEAM: Banks, Moore, Wilson, Butcher, J Charlton, B Charlton, Bremner, Brooking, Best, Keegan, Law.
BEST ALL TIME INTERNATIONAL TEAM: Yashin, Krol, Marinho, Alberto, Facchetti, Neeskens, Riveliono, Rivera, Cruyff, Pele, Di Stefano.
FAVOURITE AWAY GROUND: Arsenal.
FAVOURITE FOREIGN STADIUM: San Bernabeau, Madrid, and Feyenoord, Rotterdam.
BEST GOAL I'VE SCORED: The volley I hit against Birmingham last season when Clive Woods' corner was headed to the edge of the box.
BEST GOAL SEEN SCORED: Frank Worthington's side foot volley for Bolton v Man City on TV last season. Simple, but brilliant.
MOST DIFFICULT OPPONENT: Gerry Gow, of Bristol City — he's hard but fair.
MOST MEMORABLE MATCH: We beat PSV Eindhoven pre-season and we've never played so well. We won 3-1.
MY MAGIC MOMENT IN FOOTBALL: Playing for Twente in 1978 when we beat PEC 3-0 and my first cap against a Dutch League Foreign players XI.
MISCELLANEOUS LIKES: Music, driving my car, playing with my children.
MISCELLANEOUS DISLIKES: Smoking and long coach journeys.
FAVOURITE TV SHOW: Benny Hill and sport.
TV SHOW I ALWAYS SWITCH OFF: Programmes between 6 and 7pm on Sundays.
FAVOURITE MUSICIANS/SINGERS: Elton John, Eagles, Wings, Billy Joel.
FAVOURITE FOOD: Spaghetti.
FAVOURITE DRINK: Milk.
BEST COUNTRIES VISITED: Spain, Greece.
FAVOURITE FILM ACTOR/ACTRESS: Clint Eastwood, Steve McQueen, Susan George.
BEST FILM SEEN THIS YEAR: Escape from Alcatraz.
BIGGEST INFLUENCE ON CAREER: My parents.
WHAT DON'T YOU LIKE ABOUT FOOTBALL: Losing
PRE-MATCH MEAL: Boiled chicken.
INTERNATIONAL HONOURS: Two caps for Holland.
PERSONAL AMBITION: Staying healthy.
PROFESSIONAL AMBITION: To play at Wembley.
CAREER AFTER PLAYING: I won't stay in football when I retire, but I will return to Holland.
PLAYERS FOR THE FUTURE: Terry Butcher and Russell Osman of Ipswich.
WHO WOULD YOU MOST LIKE TO MEET: Paul McCartney.
ADVICE TO YOUNGSTERS: Always heed advice.

1980-81

Keegan heads home, Ricky Villa's wonder goal and a plastic pitch.

1980-81

ENGLAND'S NO.1?

August 2, 1980
There's no splitting England goalkeepers Peter Shilton and Ray Clemence in the MATCH poll. 15-year-old Paul Phillipson reckons Clemence is 'as fast as a falcon', while Simon Bosson from Oldham says Shilts has got 'elastic legs'.

'BEEFY' BOTHAM!

September 6, 1980
West Brom striker Cyrille Regis teaches readers how to head the ball in the MATCH Soccer School. Ian Botham talks of his love for Chelsea and playing for Fourth Division Scunthorpe, while Kevin Keegan reveals his three greatest goals.

MAN IN THE MASK!

September 20, 1980
Stoke defender Alan Dodd welcomes MATCH into his Staffordshire home as we meet his goat Looby-Loo and setters Red and Randy. Alan also shows off his antique collection of helmets and breastplates in 'The Other World Of...'

KENNY'S STORY!

January 17, 1981
Teenage Norwich striker Justin Fashanu signs for MATCH, revealing that he reached two amateur heavyweight boxing finals before turning to football. A 'super colour picture strip' about the life of Liverpool's Kenny Dalglish begins.

CURRIE ON CARPET!

July 11, 1981
QPR's midfield maestro Tony Currie describes the benefits of the new £350,000 Loftus Road 'Omniturf' pitch, while Phil Neal and Arthur Albiston give their views on the introduction of the three points for a win system.

John Wark

» STAR PLAYERS!

JOHN WARK, Ipswich: The Scottish midfielder helped Bobby Robson's side push Aston Villa all the way in the title race. He scored an incredible 36 goals, 14 on the way to the UEFA Cup final, and ended the season with a role in the film 'Escape To Victory'.

GARY SHAW, Aston Villa: The blond striker formed a deadly strikeforce with Peter Withe, netting the goals that took Villa to their first title in 71 years.

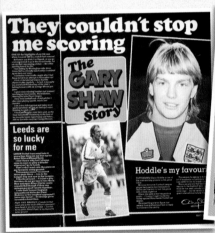

Tottenham's white home kit.

Sunderland's dodgy away kit.

>> SEASON HIGHLIGHTS!

AUGUST: Journeyman striker Peter Withe joins Division One hopefuls Aston Villa for £500,000 from Newcastle.

SEPTEMBER: England beat Norway 4-0 in their first qualifying game for the 1982 World Cup.

OCTOBER: Liverpool thrash Finnish part-timers Oulu Palloseura 10-1 in the first round of the European Cup.

NOVEMBER: Man. City splash out £220,000 on last season's Division One top scorer, Southampton's Phil Boyer.

DECEMBER: Arsenal beat Man. United 2-1 in a massive top-of-the-table clash at Highbury.

JANUARY: A Kevin Keegan inspired Southampton climb to fourth in the table after beating Sunderland 2-1.

FEBRUARY: Nottingham Forest are hammered by UEFA with a £4,000 fine after displaying shirt sponsors during a European tie.

MARCH: Ipswich's 3-0 win over Tottenham is Bobby Robson's side's sixth straight league victory and keeps them top of Division One.

APRIL: Aston Villa seal their first League title for 71 years, having used only 14 players in the whole season.

MAY: The European Cup is lifted by an English club for the fifth season in a row. Liverpool beat Real Madrid 1-0 in Paris with Alan Kennedy scoring the only goal of the game.

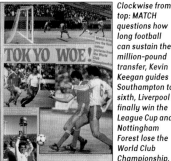

Clockwise from top: MATCH questions how long football can sustain the million-pound transfer, Kevin Keegan guides Southampton to sixth, Liverpool finally win the League Cup and Nottingham Forest lose the World Club Championship.

>> RISING STARS!

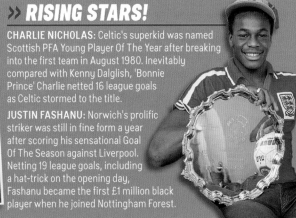

CHARLIE NICHOLAS: Celtic's superkid was named Scottish PFA Young Player Of The Year after breaking into the first team in August 1980. Inevitably compared with Kenny Dalglish, 'Bonnie Prince' Charlie netted 16 league goals as Celtic stormed to the title.

JUSTIN FASHANU: Norwich's prolific striker was still in fine form a year after scoring his sensational Goal Of The Season against Liverpool. Netting 19 league goals, including a hat-trick on the opening day, Fashanu became the first £1 million black player when he joined Nottingham Forest.

>> FINAL LEAGUE TABLES!

DIVISION ONE

	CLUB	P	W	D	L	F	A	GD	Pts
1	Aston Villa	42	26	8	8	72	40	+32	60
2	Ipswich	42	23	10	9	77	43	+34	56
3	Arsenal	42	19	15	8	61	45	+16	53
4	West Brom	42	20	12	10	60	42	+18	52
5	Liverpool	42	17	17	8	62	42	+20	51
6	Southampton	42	20	10	12	76	56	+20	50
7	Nott'm Forest	42	19	12	11	62	44	+18	50
8	Man. United	42	15	18	9	51	36	+15	48
9	Leeds	42	17	10	15	39	47	-8	44
10	Tottenham	42	14	15	13	70	68	+2	43
11	Stoke	42	12	12	18	51	60	-9	42
12	Man. City	42	14	11	17	56	59	-3	39
13	Birmingham	42	13	12	17	50	61	-11	38
14	Middlesbrough	42	16	5	21	53	61	-8	37
15	Everton	42	13	10	19	55	58	-3	36
16	Coventry	42	13	10	19	48	68	-20	36
17	Sunderland	42	14	7	21	52	53	-1	35
18	Wolves	42	13	9	20	43	55	-12	35
19	Brighton	42	14	7	21	54	67	-13	35
20	Norwich	42	13	7	22	49	73	-24	33
21	Leicester	42	13	6	23	40	67	-27	32
22	Crystal Palace	42	6	7	29	47	83	-36	19

TOP SCORER: Steve Archibald Tottenham, 20 goals

DIVISION TWO

	CLUB	P	W	D	L	F	A	GD	Pts
1	West Ham	42	28	10	4	79	29	+50	66
2	Notts County	42	18	17	7	49	38	+11	53
3	Swansea	42	18	14	10	64	44	+20	50
4	Blackburn	42	16	18	8	42	29	+13	50
5	Luton	42	18	12	12	61	46	+15	48
6	Derby	42	15	15	12	57	52	+5	45
7	Grimsby	42	15	13	14	44	42	+2	43
8	QPR	42	15	13	14	56	46	+10	43
9	Watford	42	16	11	15	50	45	+5	43
10	Sheff. Wed.	42	17	8	17	53	51	+2	42
11	Newcastle	42	14	14	14	30	45	-15	42
12	Chelsea	42	14	12	16	46	41	+5	40
13	Cambridge	42	17	6	19	53	65	-12	40
14	Shrewsbury	42	11	17	14	46	47	-1	39
15	Oldham	42	12	15	15	39	48	-9	39
16	Wrexham	42	12	14	16	43	45	-2	38
17	Orient	42	13	12	17	52	56	-4	38
18	Bolton	42	14	10	18	61	66	-5	38
19	Cardiff	42	12	12	18	44	60	-16	36
20	Preston	42	11	14	17	41	62	-21	36
21	Bristol City	42	7	16	19	29	51	-22	30
22	Bristol Rovers	42	5	13	24	34	65	-31	23

TOP SCORER: David Cross West Ham, 22 goals

DIVISION THREE

	CLUB	P	W	D	L	F	A	GD	Pts
1	Rotherham	46	24	13	9	62	32	+30	61
2	Barnsley	46	21	17	8	72	45	+27	59
3	Charlton	46	25	9	12	63	44	+19	59
4	Huddersfield	46	21	14	11	71	40	+31	56
5	Chesterfield	46	23	10	13	72	48	+24	56
6	Portsmouth	46	22	9	15	55	47	+8	53
7	Plymouth	46	19	14	13	56	44	+12	52
8	Burnley	46	18	14	14	60	48	+12	50
9	Brentford	46	14	19	13	52	49	+3	47
10	Reading	46	18	10	18	62	62	0	46
11	Exeter	46	16	13	17	62	66	-4	45
12	Newport	46	15	13	18	64	61	+3	43
13	Fulham	46	15	13	18	57	64	-7	43
14	Oxford	46	13	17	16	39	47	-8	43
15	Gillingham	46	12	18	16	48	58	-10	42
16	Millwall	46	14	14	18	43	60	-17	42
17	Swindon	46	13	15	18	51	56	-5	41
18	Chester	46	15	11	20	38	48	-10	41
19	Carlisle	46	14	13	19	56	70	-14	41
20	Walsall	46	13	15	18	59	74	-15	41
21	Sheff. United	46	14	12	20	65	63	+2	40
22	Colchester	46	14	11	21	45	65	-20	39
23	Blackpool	46	9	14	23	45	75	-30	32
24	Hull	46	8	16	22	40	71	-31	32

TOP SCORER: Tony Kellow Exeter, 25 goals

DIVISION FOUR

	CLUB	P	W	D	L	F	A	GD	Pts
1	Southend	46	30	7	9	79	31	+48	67
2	Lincoln	46	25	15	6	66	25	+41	65
3	Doncaster	46	22	12	12	59	49	+10	56
4	Wimbledon	46	23	9	14	64	46	+18	55
5	Peterborough	46	17	18	11	68	54	+14	52
6	Aldershot	46	18	14	14	43	41	+2	50
7	Mansfield	46	20	9	17	58	44	+14	49
8	Darlington	46	19	11	16	65	59	+6	49
9	Hartlepool	46	20	9	17	64	61	+3	49
10	Northampton	46	18	13	15	65	67	-2	49
11	Wigan	46	18	11	17	51	55	-4	47
12	Bury	46	17	11	18	70	62	+8	45
13	Bournemouth	46	16	13	17	47	48	-1	45
14	Bradford	46	14	16	16	53	60	-7	44
15	Rochdale	46	14	15	17	60	70	-10	43
16	Scunthorpe	46	11	20	15	60	69	-9	42
17	Torquay	46	18	5	23	55	63	-8	41
18	Crewe	46	13	14	19	48	61	-13	40
19	Port Vale	46	12	15	19	57	70	-13	39
20	Stockport	46	16	7	23	44	57	-13	39
21	Tranmere	46	13	10	23	59	73	-14	36
22	Hereford	46	11	13	22	38	62	-24	35
23	Halifax	46	11	12	23	44	71	-27	34
24	York	46	12	9	25	47	66	-19	33

TOP SCORER: Alan Cork Wimbledon, 23 goals

THE GOAL THAT

THE

* * * * * * * * *
Viva Villa

TEARS of despair turned to tears of joy for bearded-Argentinian Ricky Villa as the Spurs went marching in to lift the trophy in the 100th FA Cup Final.

For it was Villa - so often overshadowed by his fellow countryman and team-mate Ossie Ardiles - who became the most unlikely of heroes in this the 'Year of the Cockerel'.

Off-form and finally substituted in Spurs first Wembley clash with gallant Manchester City, Villa rose to the replay to score two goals - the second and eventual match-winner, one of the best ever to grace the famous Wembley turf.

And that brilliant individual goal, which made the score 3-2 and had everyone in the stadium on their feet in admiration, is captured here in the marvellous pictures of Match photographer DUNCAN CUBITT.

Left: Osvaldo Ardiles lunges in but fails to stop this first-half effort from City's Dave Bennett.

* * * * * * * * *

"I WAS so pleased for Ricky Villa. Steve Mackenzie's volley for City was a great goal but Ricky's winner was fantastic — one of the best goals I have ever seen." — Spurs midfielder GLENN HODDLE.

SEE Glenn's column later in this issue.

"I JOKED with the lads before the game that they'd see my name in lights at Wembley — and they did when I scored our second goal.

It's been an unbelievable season for me. To think that this time last year I was in Majorca on tour with Stoke City." — Spurs striker GARTH CROOKS.

"I WANTED to score a goal but I think I was a little lucky, having two defenders so close to me," — Spurs replay hero RICKY VILLA.

"I WAS conscious of the fact that Spurs had won all their five previous FA Cup finals, but I think we were worthy winners in the end," — Spurs skipper STEVE PERRYMAN.

"I HAVE always wanted to play at Wembley and I have now played in two finals. To win the cup is marvellous," — Spurs midfielder OSSIE ARDILES.

Right: Jubilant Spurs defender Chris Hughton with the Cup and flanked by Paul Miller and Graham Roberts.

Far right: Garth Crooks hurdles this challenge from City's young defender Nicky Reid.

WON CUP

Spurs 3
Man City 2

COVER PICTURE:

The magic moment when Spurs captain Steve Perryman lifted the F.A. Cup. Now turn to the centre pages for our super colour pictures from Wembley.

Peter Withe rises high to head Villa's second goal in their 3-0 win over Middlesbrough. It was great to finish our home programme in style, says Dennis.

Villa's

A CHAMPION

SCORING against my boyhood idols Liverpool realised a lifelong ambition . . . but the win against the former League Champions was also the turning point in Aston Villa's title assault.

The Villa players knew that our game against the mighty Reds was make or break.

If we were to make any headway in the Championship we had to beat Liverpool at Villa Park that Saturday in November.

Not only did we win . . . we won in style!

It was then I realised that the First Division Championship was within Aston Villa's grasp for the first time in 71 years.

That was one of the best days of the season for me. I scored — a goal I still remember vividly — and we gained revenge for our 2-1 defeat earlier in the season at Anfield.

But the season was punctuated with many other highlights . . .

Here are some of the games that stick out in the memory on our road to the title . . .

Learned from defeat

September 13: We lost 2-0 at home to Everton. Yes, I believe that defeat was a highspot because it made the team realise what concentration and effort was needed to win the hardest league in the world.

We took Sunderland apart

October 4: Sunderland, newly promoted to the First Division, came to Villa Park full of confidence.

We took them apart with goals from Allan Evans (2), Tony Morley and Gary Shaw.

Coppell helped us!

March 14: Drew 3-3 with Manchester United. It wasn't our performance that sticks out in my mind, although the game was a cracker.

It was Steve Coppell's comments after the match which helped us win the League.

He said Villa 'lacked the killer instinct'. We stuck his criticism — along with all the others — on a notice board at our training headquarters.

We looked at them daily and were determined to prove the people wrong.

Finished in style

April 25: Villa finished their home programme in style with a 3-0 win over Middlesbrough. Despite the gale force winds and driving rain we proved to people that we deserved the title.

We know we deserve it

May 2: A day of mixed emotions for the team. We were crowned champions but got beaten 2-0 at Arsenal.

Many players felt the tension of the occasion, but the Championship is won over 42 games and not one.

We won more games than the rest of the First Division so we knew we deserved the title.

Not enough credit

There weren't that many lowspots to our season although we were very disappointed to lose both our matches against Ipswich.

On both occasions we felt we were the better team and we gave them victory at Villa Park through two terrible defensive mistakes.

A lot of people wanted Ipswich to win the Championship and it annoys me that we haven't received the credit we earned.

But in many ways the fact so many people tipped the Suffolk side helped us — it took the limelight away from us and we were able to get on with the job of winning matches.

● Next week I'll be telling you about the players who helped Villa to championship glory and our hopes for next season. See you then!

HOW THE TITLE WAS WON

Villa's complete League record for the season.

DATE	OPPONENTS	RESULT	SCORERS	GATE
Aug 16:	Leeds (A)	2-1	Morley, Shaw	23,401
Aug 20:	Norwich (H)	1-0	Shaw	25,970
Aug 23:	Man City (A)	2-2	Withe 2	30,017
Aug 30:	Coventry (H)	1-0	Shaw	26,050
Sept 6:	Ipswich (A)	0-1		23,192
Sept 13:	Everton (H)	0-2		25,673
Sept 20:	Wolves (H)	2-1	Hughes og, Geddis	26,881
Sept 27:	Crystal Pal (A)	1-0	Shaw	18,398
Oct 4:	Sunderland (H)	4-0	Evans 2, Morley, Shaw	26,914
Oct 8:	Man Utd (A)	3-3	Withe, Cowans pen, Shaw	38,831
Oct 11:	Birmingham (A)	2-1	Cowans pen, Evans	33,879
Oct 18:	Spurs (H)	3-0	Morley 2, Withe	30,940
Oct 22:	Brighton (H)	4-1	Mortimer, Withe, Bremner, Shaw	27,367
Oct 25:	Southampton (A)	2-1	Morley, Withe	21,249
Nov 1:	Leicester (H)	2-0	Shaw, Cowans	29,953
Nov 8:	West Brom (A)	0-0		34,001
Nov 12:	Norwich (A)	3-1	Shaw 2, Evans	17,050
Nov 15:	Leeds (H)	1-1	Shaw	29,106
Nov 22:	Liverpool (A)	1-2	Evans	48,114
Nov 29:	Arsenal (H)	1-1	Morley	30,140
Dec 6:	Middlesbro (A)	1-2	Shaw	15,597
Dec 13:	Birmingham (H)	3-0	Geddis 2, Shaw	41,101
Dec 20:	Brighton (A)	0-1		16,425
Dec 26:	Stoke (H)	1-0	Withe	34,658
Dec 27:	Nottm For (A)	2-2	Lloyd og, Shaw	33,930
Jan 10:	Liverpool (H)	2-0	Withe, Mortimer	47,960
Jan 17:	Coventry (A)	2-1	Morley, Withe	27,020
Jan 31:	Man City (H)	1-0	Shaw	33,682
Feb 7:	Everton (A)	3-1	Morley, Mortimer, Cowans	31,434
Feb 21:	Crystal Pal (H)	2-1	Withe 2	27,203
Feb 28:	Wolves (A)	1-0	Withe	34,693
Mar 7:	Sunderland (A)	2-1	Evans, Mortimer	27,278
Mar 14:	Man Utd (H)	3-3	Withe 2, Shaw	42,182
Mar 21:	Spurs (A)	0-2		35,091
Mar 28:	Southampton (H)	2-1	Morley, Geddis	32,467
April 4:	Leicester (A)	4-2	Withe 2, Bremner, Morley	26,032
April 8:	West Brom (H)	1-0	Withe	47,998
April 14:	Ipswich (H)	1-2	Shaw	47,494
April 18:	Nottm For (H)	2-0	Cowans pen, Withe	34,707
April 20:	Stoke (A)	1-1	Withe	23,500
April 25:	Middlesbro (H)	3-0	Shaw, Withe, Evans	38,018
May 2:	Arsenal (A)	0-2		57,472

● Villa's results first in each case.

oad to glory

DIARY BY DENNIS MORTIMER

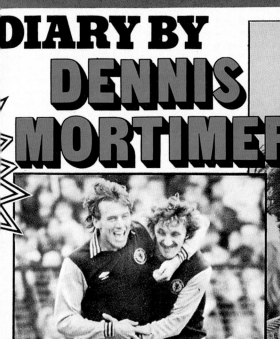

In championship mood — Tony Morley (left), Villa's third top scorer in the League, and Scots midfielder Des Bremner.

GOALSCORERS

Peter Withe	
Gary Shaw	20
Tony Morley	18
Allan Evans	10
Gordon Cowans	7
Dennis Mortimer	5
David Geddis	4
Des Bremner	4
Own goals	2
Total	2
	72

3 Points for a WIN

PHIL NEAL
(Liverpool and England)

"THREE points for a win? . . . Oh, yes, I'd forgotten about that with still six weeks to go before we start. Should be very interesting.

"There'll be a lot of close attention to the tables early on but I'm bound to say it's unlikely to make much difference to Liverpool.

"We don't need the extra incentive to win matches!

"But, it could certainly make a difference to how the likes of Stoke and Leeds approach their matches. They are known for keeping it tight as draw specialists but this new system could bring them out and that should be good for the game and the fans.

"I expect the points will also prove significant towards the end of the season, too and instead of teams, settling for a point when they are hit by injuries, instead they'll have to gamble on attack for a point for promotion or to stay up.

"I'm looking forward to seeing how it works."

Left: Phil Neal of European champions Liverpool and England — 'We don't need any extra incentive to win matches at Liverpool!'

ARTHUR ALBISTON
(Manchester United)

"I'M not sure awarding three points for a win is the answer.

"The idea is to get away teams coming out and attacking the home side, but with three points at stake both the home side and the away side are going to want to hold on if they go a goal up.

"I think we have to try new ideas but I don't think the game is as bad as some of the critics would have us believe.

"Gates have gone down, but I think it's chiefly due to the fact people can't afford to watch so much football."

IAN MELLOR
(Sheffield Wednesday)

"I CAN'T see the new system making much difference at all.

"It just means that teams who are ahead will be even more determined to keep their lead knowing that there is an extra point at stake.

"I would have preferred a points for goals scheme where a side got extra points for scoring over three goals in a match — that would have encouraged teams to go forward."

COLIN LEE
(Chelsea)

"I THINK it's quite a good idea because it should make managers more attack minded . . . especially if they need the points.

"It will probably have the greatest effect towards the end of the season when points become vital.

"It's going to be very important for the home sides to win matches.

"Generally speaking I don't think we have anything to lose by giving it a try — I'm all for trying to win back some of the missing fans."

DO YOU agree with the stars about the new three points for a win system? Send your views to: Terrace Talk, Match Weekly, Midgate House, Midgate, Peterborough.

BILLY ASHCROFT
(Middlesbrough)

"ENTERTAINING football should soar next season with the new points system.

"Something needed to be done and I think the three points for a win will help bring back the fans.

"I'm looking forward to the experiment. Teams will have to change their style of play because it will be no use them going for a draw when there's three points up for grabs if you win.

"Anything that promotes entertaining football has got to be good for the game."

SALUTE KING KENNEDY

LIVERPOOL are Champions of Europe yet again and this is the moment (above) that clinched it.

With eighty-three tense, goalless minutes gone, Alan Kennedy stormed into the Real Madrid area, chesting down a throw-in from namesake Ray Kennedy and brushing aside the challenge of Garcia Cortes before lashing this left foot shot past goalkeeper Agustin.

It was an unforgettable moment and one which 12,000 loyal Liverpool fans in the Parc Des Princes stadium in Paris rose to salute.

Minutes later Liverpool captain Phil Thompson, also pictured holding off the challenge of Madrid's brilliant British import Laurie Cunningham, hoisted Liverpool's third European Champions trophy aloft.

What a night of celebration followed and it continued the following day as thousands of Merseysiders cheered home their heroes in a parade through the streets of Liverpool.

LIVERPOOL (0) 1
A. Kennedy 83

Att: 48,360

REAL MADRID (0) 0

Receipts: £275,000

Liverpool: Clemence 6, Neal 7, Kennedy A 7, Thompson 7, *KENNEDY R 8, Hansen 7, Dalglish 6 (sub Case), Lee 7, Johnson 6, McDermott 7, Sourness 7.
Real Madrid: *AGUSTIN 7, Cortes 5, Camacho 6, Stielike 6, Sabido 6 (sub Pineda), Del Bosque 6, Juanito 6, Angel 5, Santillana 5, Navajas 6, Cunningham 5.
Referee: L. Palotai (Hungary).

Match Rating:**

● **COLOUR PICTURE** (over the page): It's hats off to Liverpool and goalscorer Alan Kennedy from Phil Neal as they parade the European Cup after their victory.

MATCH weekly

PAUL BRUSH

● West Ham's Paul Brush meets his namesake Basil.

WEST HAM UNITED

match makers

FULL NAME: Paul Brush
BIRTHPLACE/BIRTHDATE: Plaistow, London, February 22, 1958
HEIGHT/WEIGHT: 5ft 11in, 11st 11lb
MARRIED: Yes to Marilyn
CHILDREN: None
CAR: Ford Fiesta 1100L
CLUB NICKNAME: Basil or Brushie
WORST EVER INJURY: Broke arm last season
FAVOURITE FOOTBALL LEAGUE PLAYER AND WHY?: Bobby Moore, masterful reader of a game
FAVOURITE FOREIGN PLAYER AND WHY?: Pele. Brilliant with all the soccer skills
BEST ALL TIME BRITISH TEAM: Banks, McGrain, Wilson, England, Moore, Ball, Souness, Best, Hurst, Greaves, R. Charlton
ALL TIME INTERNATIONAL XI: Banks (England), Kaltz (W. Germany), Ray Wilson, Moore (England), Krol (Holland), Beckenbauer (W. Germany), Rivelino (Brazil), Cruyff (Holland), Pele (Brazil), Eusebio (Portugal), Kempes (Argentina)
FAVOURITE AWAY GROUND: Portman Road
BEST GOAL SCORED: Scored the goal which put Cumberland School in to the English schools final
BEST GOAL SEEN SCORED: Mickey Walsh's solo run and shot for Blackpool against Sunderland — won Goal of the Season about five years ago
MOST DIFFICULT OPPONENT: Laurie Cunningham
MOST MEMORABLE MATCH: My debut for West Ham against Norwich, August 1977
OWN MAGIC MOMENT IN FOOTBALL: Final whistle, FA Cup semi-final replay against Everton at Elland Road, April 1980

BIGGEST DISAPPOINTMENT: Only being substitute for the FA Cup final after playing in every round
FAVOURITE OTHER SPORTS: Golf, tennis
MISCELLANEOUS LIKES: Listening to music
MISCELLANEOUS DISLIKES: Washing up, cleaning the car
FAVOURITE TV SHOW: Basil Brush Show, Soap
TV SHOW YOU ALWAYS SWITCH OFF: Dr Who
FAVOURITE READING: Comedy books, Alistair McLean
FAVOURITE MUSICIAN/SINGER: Eagles, Rod Stewart
FAVOURITE FOOD: Mixed grill
BEST COUNTRY VISITED: United States
FAVOURITE ACTOR/ACTRESS: Peter Sellers, Spike Milligan, Meryl Streep
BEST FILMS SEEN IN PAST YEARS: Ten and The Deerhunter
BEST FRIEND: My wife
BIGGEST INFLUENCE ON CAREER: My parents
WHAT DON'T YOU LIKE ABOUT FOOTBALL: Losing and injuries
SUPERSTITION: Always put my shorts on last
PRE MATCH MEAL: Beans on toast
PERSONAL AMBITION: To be happy
PROFESSIONAL AMBITION: To be one of the outstanding full backs in the country
A PLAYER FOR THE FUTURE: Graham Rix will become world class
WHO WOULD YOU MOST LIKE TO MEET?: As you can see I've already met Basil Brush, so I'll settle for Rod Stewart

Paul Brush

1981-82

*Robson's record, Paolo Rossi
and Maradona arrives.*

1981-82

PLAY MASTERMIND!

August 29, 1981

MATCH kicks off the new season with the first of three 7" 'Mastermind Of Soccer' quiz discs. Division One stars Peter Withe, Glenn Hoddle and Alan Kennedy join quizmaster Mike Ingham on the free records.

CROOKS CRACKER!

April 24, 1982

Spurs striker Garth Crooks must have been wearing the smallest shorts of all time when he netted his FA Cup semi-final gem against Leicester. Mark Hateley thinks he's dreaming after a brace on his England U-21 debut.

DODGY PERM!

March 13, 1982

Graeme Souness, complete with mega perm, tries to out-smile Glenn Hoddle in this classic cover. Bruce Grobbelaar speaks of his first Wembley appearance, while Ray Clemence prepares to face his old Anfield team-mates.

VIVA ESPANA!

June 26, 1982

The first images from the World Cup in Spain appear in MATCH Weekly as the tournament opens in the Nou Camp. Bryan Robson bags his first goal after just 27 seconds, and puts England on their way to the second round.

FAB AT 40!

July 17, 1982

Dino Zoff is 40 years young as he lifts the World Cup for Italy. Paolo Rossi's deadly finishing wraps up the Golden Boot and Marco Tardelli's memorable goal celebration is on show as Italy beat West Germany 3-1 in The Bernabeu.

Kevin Keegan

Steve Moran

>> STAR PLAYERS!

KEVIN KEEGAN, Southampton: He may have been in the twilight of a brilliant career, but you would never have noticed after a stunning season with The Saints. The former European Player Of The Year scored 26 goals to help Southampton to an impressive seventh place. That summer saw him travel to Spain as part of England's World Cup squad.

STEVE MORAN, Southampton: The Saints striker was all set to hit the big-time in 1981, and had netted ten times before the turn of the year when injury struck. But he'd already done enough after some sparkling displays alongside Kevin Keegan.

BEST KIT!

Swansea's all-white home kit.

WORST KIT!

Coventry's Talbot home kit.

>> SEASON HIGHLIGHTS!

AUGUST: Arsenal sign a three-year sponsorship deal worth £400,000 with electronics company JVC.

SEPTEMBER: QPR become the first British club to play on a 'plastic pitch', losing their first home game 2-1 to Luton.

OCTOBER: Man. United break the British transfer record, paying £1.5 million for West Brom and England midfielder Bryan Robson.

NOVEMBER: Ipswich's 2-0 defeat at Stoke is the first time the East Anglian side fail to score in a league game for seven months.

DECEMBER: Only eight league games survive the bad weather as the Boxing Day fixtures are decimated.

JANUARY: Aberdeen manager Alex Ferguson turns down the Wolves hot-seat, preferring to stay at Pittodrie.

FEBRUARY: Aston Villa boss Ron Saunders quits the club, leaving Tony Barton in temporary charge of the Midlands side.

MARCH: Brighton beat Liverpool 1-0 at Anfield. The Reds bounce back by winning their next 11 league games.

APRIL: Man. United give a league debut to 16-year-old Northern Ireland forward Norman Whiteside.

MAY: Aston Villa beat Bayern Munich 1-0 to win the European Cup.

JUNE: Italy lift a third World Cup, their first for 44 years.

Clockwise from top: Bryan Robson signs for Man. United on the Old Trafford pitch, Trevor Francis stays for a season at Maine Road, Ronnie Whelan scores twice in the League Cup final and Bruce Grobbelaar takes over from Ray Clemence.

>> RISING STARS!

BRYAN ROBSON: What a season for 'Captain Marvel'. As if breaking the British transfer record wasn't enough, he then scored the fastest ever World Cup goal. A feat that was only bettered by Turkey's Hakan Sukur 20 years later.

DIEGO MARADONA: The Boca Juniors superstar broke on to the world stage at Spain '82, scoring twice against Hungary and being sent off against Brazil. Barcelona then bought him for a world-record £5 million.

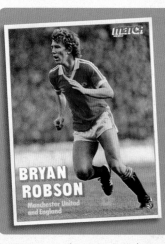

BRYAN ROBSON
Manchester United and England

>> FINAL LEAGUE TABLES!

DIVISION ONE

	CLUB	P	W	D	L	F	A	GD	Pts
1	Liverpool	42	26	9	7	80	32	+48	87
2	Ipswich	42	26	5	11	75	53	+22	83
3	Man. United	42	22	12	8	59	29	+30	78
4	Tottenham	42	20	11	11	67	48	+19	71
5	Arsenal	42	20	11	11	48	37	+11	71
6	Swansea	42	21	6	15	58	51	+7	69
7	Southampton	42	19	9	14	72	67	+5	66
8	Everton	42	17	13	12	56	50	+6	64
9	West Ham	42	14	16	12	66	57	+9	58
10	Man. City	42	15	13	14	49	50	-1	58
11	Aston Villa	42	15	12	15	55	53	+2	57
12	Nott'm Forest	42	15	12	15	42	48	-6	57
13	Brighton	42	13	13	16	43	52	-9	52
14	Coventry	42	13	11	18	56	62	-6	50
15	Notts County	42	13	8	21	61	69	-8	47
16	Birmingham	42	10	14	18	53	61	-8	44
17	West Brom	42	11	11	20	46	57	-11	44
18	Stoke	42	12	8	22	44	63	-19	44
19	Sunderland	42	11	11	20	38	58	-20	44
20	Leeds	42	10	12	20	39	61	-22	42
21	Wolves	42	10	10	22	32	63	-31	40
22	Middlesbrough	42	8	15	19	34	52	-18	39

TOP SCORER: Kevin Keegan Southampton, 26 goals

DIVISION TWO

	CLUB	P	W	D	L	F	A	GD	Pts
1	Luton	42	25	13	4	86	46	+40	88
2	Watford	42	23	11	8	76	42	+34	80
3	Norwich	42	22	5	15	64	50	+14	71
4	Sheff. Wed.	42	20	10	12	55	51	+4	70
5	QPR	42	21	6	15	65	43	+22	69
6	Barnsley	42	19	10	13	59	41	+18	67
7	Rotherham	42	20	7	15	66	54	+12	67
8	Leicester	42	18	12	12	56	48	+8	66
9	Newcastle	42	18	8	16	52	50	+2	62
10	Blackburn	42	16	11	15	47	43	+4	59
11	Oldham	42	15	14	13	50	51	-1	59
12	Chelsea	42	15	12	15	60	60	0	57
13	Charlton	42	13	12	17	50	65	-15	51
14	Cambridge	42	13	9	20	48	53	-5	48
15	Crystal Palace	42	13	9	20	34	45	-11	48
16	Derby	42	12	12	18	53	68	-15	48
17	Grimsby	42	11	13	18	53	65	-12	46
18	Shrewsbury	42	11	13	18	37	57	-20	46
19	Bolton	42	13	7	22	39	61	-22	46
20	Cardiff	42	12	8	22	45	61	-16	44
21	Wrexham	42	11	11	20	40	56	-16	44
22	Orient	42	9	12	21	36	61	-25	39

TOP SCORER: Ronnie Moore Rotherham, 22 goals

DIVISION THREE

	CLUB	P	W	D	L	F	A	GD	Pts
1	Burnley	46	21	17	8	66	45	+21	80
2	Carlisle	46	23	11	12	65	50	+15	80
3	Fulham	46	21	15	10	77	51	+26	78
4	Lincoln	46	21	14	11	66	40	+26	77
5	Oxford	46	19	14	13	63	49	+14	71
6	Gillingham	46	20	11	15	64	56	+8	71
7	Southend	46	18	15	13	63	51	+12	69
8	Brentford	46	19	11	16	56	47	+9	68
9	Millwall	46	18	13	15	62	62	0	67
10	Plymouth	46	18	11	17	64	56	+8	65
11	Chesterfield	46	18	10	18	57	58	-1	64
12	Reading	46	17	11	18	67	75	-8	62
13	Portsmouth	46	14	19	13	56	51	+5	61
14	Preston	46	16	13	17	50	56	-6	61
15	Bristol Rovers*	46	18	9	19	58	65	-7	61
16	Newport	46	14	16	16	54	54	0	58
17	Huddersfield	46	15	12	19	64	59	+5	57
18	Exeter	46	16	9	21	71	84	-13	57
19	Doncaster	46	13	17	16	55	68	-13	56
20	Walsall	46	13	14	19	51	55	-4	53
21	Wimbledon	46	14	11	21	61	75	-14	53
22	Swindon	46	13	13	20	55	71	-16	52
23	Bristol City	46	11	13	22	40	65	-25	46
24	Chester	46	7	11	28	36	78	-42	32

TOP SCORER: Gordon Davies Fulham, 24 goals

DIVISION FOUR

	CLUB	P	W	D	L	F	A	GD	Pts
1	Sheff. United	46	27	15	4	94	41	+53	96
2	Bradford	46	26	13	7	88	45	+43	91
3	Wigan	46	26	13	7	80	46	+34	91
4	Bournemouth	46	23	19	4	62	30	+32	88
5	Peterborough	46	24	10	12	71	57	+14	82
6	Colchester	46	20	12	14	82	57	+25	72
7	Port Vale	46	18	16	12	56	49	+7	70
8	Hull	46	19	12	15	70	61	+9	69
9	Bury	46	17	17	12	80	59	+21	68
10	Hereford	46	16	19	11	64	58	+6	67
11	Tranmere	46	14	18	14	51	56	-5	60
12	Blackpool	46	13	18	15	66	60	+6	58
13	Darlington	46	15	13	18	61	62	-1	58
14	Hartlepool	46	13	16	17	73	84	-11	55
15	Torquay	46	14	13	19	47	59	-12	55
16	Aldershot	46	13	15	18	57	68	-11	54
17	York	46	14	8	24	69	91	-22	50
18	Stockport	46	12	13	21	48	67	-19	49
19	Halifax	46	9	22	15	51	72	-21	49
20	Mansfield *	46	13	10	23	63	81	-18	47
21	Rochdale	46	10	16	20	50	62	-12	46
22	Northampton	46	11	9	26	57	84	-27	42
23	Scunthorpe	46	9	15	22	43	79	-36	42
24	Crewe	46	6	9	31	29	84	-55	27

TOP SCORER: Keith Edwards Sheff. United, 36 goals (1 for Hull)

*Two points deducted.

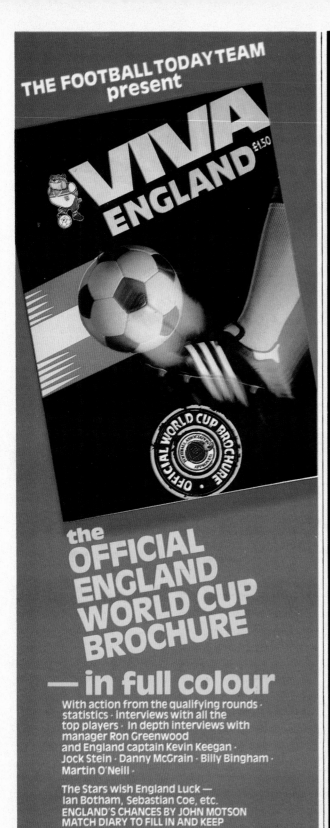
VILLA

ASTON VILLA kept the European Cup in England for a record sixth successive season on a night charged with emotion and drama.

Underdogs to Bayern Munich before the Final kicked off, Villa lost regular goalkeeper Jimmy Rimmer after just ten minutes. But that simply paved the way for young reserve 'keeper Nigel Spink — playing in only his second first team match — to turn in a heroic performance.

And when Peter Withe gave Villa the lead against the run of play in the second half it just had to be England's night again.

We've won the Cup! Gary Williams, Allan Evans and skipper Dennis Mortimer make the happiest of trios as they pose with their prize.

It's there! The ball is in the net, goalscorer Peter Withe is in the air and Bayern goalkeeper Muller is on his knees as Villa grab their European Cup winner.

SIX - HITTERS!

Bayern Munich star Karl-Heinz Rummenigge is halted by full-back Gary Williams' tackle.

What a moment for 23-year-old reserve goalkeeper Nigel Spink (right) as he raises the giant trophy. He was Villa's unlikeliest hero in what was only his second first team game!

CUP FINAL 82

Left: Penalty! Spurs' Graham Roberts is felled by a tackle from Tony Currie following a tremendous run into the Rangers box.
Above: Glenn Hoddle sends goalkeeper Peter Hucker the wrong way from the penalty spot to score the Cup-winning goal.

The victorious Spurs team line up with the FA Cup prior to taking off on their lap of honour round Wembley.

HIT-MAN

Glenn's to rob

HOT-shot Glenn Hoddle was spot-on to take the F Cup to White Hart Lane fo the second year in succession.

The 'Match' columnist' sixth minute penalty in th Final replay against QPR proved to be the match-winner . . . and so brought Spurs just rewar for their long and courageous campaign in what was their 66th matc

The expression on the face of Spurs skipper Steve Perryman says it all as he holds the FA Cup aloft for the second year running.

HODDLE

We've won the Cup! Match-winner Glenn Hoddle (wearing Gary Waddock's Rangers shirt) and striker Steve Archibald raise the prized silverware.

spot-on Rangers

. . . the season.
Brave underdogs
Rangers from the Second
Division made Tottenham
battle all the way and the
Spurs style, which has
packed in the fans this
season, was missing as
they hung on desperately.
But no neutral fan could
deny Keith Burkinshaw's
men their moment of
glory . . . captured in this
Wembley colour special.

MATCH Weekly has done it again! Against all the odds, we bring you the VERY FIRST colour pictures from the World Cup Final.

A twin-engined Commanche aircraft, chartered especially by Match Weekly, flew out to Madrid to collect the films on Sunday night.

And in a dramatic race against the clock the pictures arrived back in time to appear EXCLUSIVELY FOR OUR READERS in this issue (see front cover and centre pages).

Together with inside stories capturing the immediate reactions of the new World Champions and views from top players in this country, it all adds up to an unrivalled coverage of soccer's greatest spectacle.

ITALY ON TOP

ITALIAN manager Enzo Bearzot was managing to smile, talk, laugh and smoke his famous pipe all at the same time claiming: "This is the happiest day of my life."

Goalscoring hero Paolo Rossi was dancing around minus one boot and telling everyone: "I'm so happy. So very happy."

And all Bruno Conti could muster was: "What a stadium. What a match. What can I say?"

Italy were being hailed the Champions of the World and no-one could deny them their moment of glory.

Winners of soccer's greatest prize in 1934 and 1938, they clinched the hat-trick against all the critics and all the odds.

They entered the Final against West Germany already minus influential midfielder Giancarlo Antognoni and lost striker Francesco Graziani after just seven minutes.

Then after 24 minutes they squandered a marvellous chance to take the lead when Antonio Cabrini became the first man to miss a penalty in a World Cup Final.

Nothing it seemed was going right for the team which had come under heavy fire from the Italian Press before the tournament even kicked off.

But Paolo Rossi — the man the critics had said should never have even been included in the squad — set the seal on one of football's most amazing comebacks by scoring the goal which put the Italian's on the road to glory.

Once he had broken the deadlock in the 57th minute with his sixth goal of the tournament his side went on to overwhelm their German opponents.

A marvellous second from Marco Tardelli eleven minutes later and a third from Allessandro Altobelli ten minutes from time ensured the gold prize was Italy-bound.

While Paul Breitner pulled a goal back for Germany there was to be no repeat of their famous 'Houdini' act of the Semi-Finals.

And so it was left to Italy's skipper Dino Zoff — at 40 years of age the oldest World Cup winner in history — to lift the precious trophy high above his head to a crescendo of noise inside Madrid's famous Bernabeu Stadium.

Said Zoff: "I may be 40, but I feel like a youngster. I plan to carry on playing for a while longer yet!

"This win is not only for us — it is for our families and friends and everyone in Italy."

Claudio Gentile, minus the moustache he shaved off in honour of Italy reaching the Semi-Finals, said: "It's marvellous. It shows all our critics that we know how to play football and we are the best."

Revolution

Added Marco Tardelli, voted 'Man of the Match' in the Final: "When I scored I knew there would have to be a complete revolution if Italy were not to win.

"I just felt so great. I ran over to the bench to hug all my team mates but the officials wouldn't let me.

"It didn't matter though. What counts is the victory."

Outside the stadium the scene was no less chaotic.

Italian World Cup fever was sweeping through the streets of Madrid.

Roads were jammed with hooting, flag-waving fans chanting the names of their heros.

And back home in Italy it was pandemonium. Police in Rome estimated that more than 300,000 people crowded into the city's main square — closed to traffic two hours before kick off.

Fans leapt into fountains, painted their faces red, white and green and two clowns painted a circus elephant blue before parading it across the bridges of Venice.

Even opera took second place to soccer . . . More than 20,000 people gathered in Verona for an open air performance of 'Othello' errupted in a ten-minute round of applause when World Cup victory was announced during the interval.

Back in Spain, Italian manager Enzo Bearzot was just coming down to earth — having been chaired round the pitch by the shoulders of his delighted team.

"It's the greatest and happiest day of my life," he said.

"Our team spirit won the Cup because after missing the penalty we needed all the spirit we could muster to get us back into the game.

"It was a dangerous psychological moment but we got through it.

"We were without Antognoni and then lost Graziani, but my younger players responded well and we played perfectly.

"One of the most important aspects of our win was the marking of Littbarski and Rummenigge by Gentile and Bergomi.

"They stuck to them like they were their biggest fans. They were brilliant.

"And Rossi of course took his goal as usual!"

The goal made Rossi the leading scorer in the Finals and as the tormentor of every team Italy met in the later stages he carried off two individual awards — the 4,000 dollar 'Golden Ball' trophy as the 'Man of the Finals' and the 'Golden Shoe' trophy worth 3,700 dollars as top scorer.

Rossi (25) has re-built his career from the ashes of a two-year suspension following a bribery scandal and now he has re-paid Bearzot's faith.

"I have always had confidence in him," said the Italian boss.

German manager Jupp Derwall said Italy deserved their win . . .

"They are good winners. They played well. We were tired and I think the extra time and penalties against France in the Semi-Finals took their toll on us."

It was the first time Derwall had seen his side beaten by European opposition since he took over the helm in 1978, but he said:

"I am very satisfied with the performance of my squad in the tournament.

"While we never found our real strength I am grateful to my players for their effort."

Derwall admitted that he had spent the interval arguing with defender Uli Stielike over tactics.

weekly

Vol. 3 No. 45

Editorial and Advertising:
Stirling House, Bretton,
Peterborough PE3 8DJ.
Telephone: 0733-260333.
Publicity, Circulation and Back
Issue Depts: Bretton Court,
Bretton, Peterborough PE3 8DZ.
Telephone: 0733-264666.
Published by EMAP National
Publications Ltd.
Printed by East Midland Litho
Printers, Oundle Road,
Peterborough.
© 1982 EMAP National
Publications Ltd.

Editor : Melvyn Bagnall
News Editor : Paul Stratton
Reporters : Anthony Hawkswell
Melvyn Beck
Design Editor : Philip Jarman
Production Michael Weavers
Photographer : Philip Bagnall
Editorial Secretary : Jacquie Apthorpe
Advertising : Kieran Hamill
Publicity : Chris Llewellyn

Subscriptions: Match Weekly Subscription
Dept., Competition House, Farndon Road,
Market Harborough, Leics.
Subscription rates: Inland £27. Overseas
– surface mail £28, air mail £33
(anywhere in Europe)

We are the Champions! The delighted Italian team set off on their victory lap around the Bernabeu stadium — Scirea holding the prized trophy.

Left: Goal! Antonio Cabrini and team mate Claudio Gentile top a pile of Italian players celebrating the third goal scored by Allessandro Altobelli.

OF THE WORLD

Tragedy for Antonio Cabrini as he watches his first-half penalty kick go wide of the German post. But it all came good for the Italians in the end.

"He insisted that I move him out front in the second half to give greater drive to our midfield.

"When I made the first change in the line-up and brought on Hrubesch for Dremmler he protested visibly and kept on shouting for the whole of the second half."

Stielike himself hit out at the referee: "He seemed to be wearing a blue shirt to me, but Italy played well and deserved their win.

"The trouble is that we never really had a settled, fit team. I tried all the second half to get things going our way but I couldn't — not with that referee."

Added influential midfielder Paul Breitner who has now scored in two World Cup Finals: "It was a triumph for Italy and we blame the extra-time in Seville. We fell away badly in the second half when the Italian's came on stronger. My goal just came too late."

'IT'S TIME TO MOVE ON'
Kevin Keegan exclusive —
page 6

ROSSI RISES AGAIN
Spotlight on the king of Italian football — page 7

'WORTHY WINNERS'

ITALY were heralded as worthy World Cup winners by the stars of the British game.

Manchester United and England midfield ace Ray Wilkins was delighted with the Italians' 3-1 win over West Germany. He said: "I'm a great admirer of their style of play.

"They've got the players who can come out and attack. When they do that — as in the later stages of the competition — they showed themselves capable of murdering any opposition.

"I just hope this victory encourages them to play attacking football and persuades them not to go back to their old defensive ways.

"Paolo Rossi got all the praise for Italy's victory, but for me their outstanding player was sweeper Scirea. He was one of the best players in the tournament," added Ray.

Scotland's reserve goalkeeper Jim Leighton admitted: "Italy won the World Cup the hard way. No-one can accuse them of getting to the Final easily.

"You've got to beat the best to win the competition and that's just what they did. Italy deserved to take the trophy.

"Prompted by the talented Bruno Conti, I thought the Italian midfield was tremendous against Germany. They worked so hard for each other.

"Paolo Rossi is the ideal striker. He's hardly in the game and then he'll suddenly pop up with a couple of goals.

He doesn't need second chances."

Northern Ireland and Southampton defender Chris Nicholl believes that the World Cup Finals lost much of their appeal when the brilliant Brazilians and attack-minded French were eliminated.

"I'd have loved to have seen those two teams in the Final because they were the only true attacking teams.

"Having said that Italy deserved their victory in the Final. You don't beat the likes of Brazil, Poland and West Germany without being a good side.

"The first half of the Final was a dull affair and I was expecting the worst when I sat down for the second half. In the end it turned out to be really thrilling."

Arthur Albiston, of Manchester United and Scotland, feared a dull Final, and for 45 minutes his worst expectations were realised.

"The last half-hour rescued the match and, overall, the Italians deserved their success, despite their poor start in drawing all three matches in their initial group.

"Rossi, in particular, came good in the second-half of the tournament and I was rather surprised by the goal-scoring power of the Italians."

Noel Brotherston, Blackburn Rovers' Irish international, said: "I reckon the right Final would have involved Italy and Brazil. That would have fired everyone's imagination."

KEVIN Beattie is convinced Bobby Robson is the man for the England job.

The former England defender spent 12 years at Ipswich with Bobby before being forced to quit the First Division last season through injury.

And he has no doubts that the man who signed him as a raw youngster from Carlisle and transformed him into England material is the obvious successor to Ron Greenwood.

"I've not had many dealings with Ron Greenwood, but I believe that Bobby would do just as good a job," says Kevin.

"I know I would love to play for England under Bobby because he is a great motivator and you want to play for the man.

"He's proved his ability at Ipswich over the years without spending gigantic sums of money.

"I know we haven't won the Championship in his time, but we couldn't have gone closer with a team virtually full of home-produced players.

"He is a very shrewd operator with a remarkable eye for a young talent, which has been proved over the years with the arrival of players like Russell Osman, Steve McCall, Terry Butcher, Eric Gates, John Wark and George Burley.

"He gets involved in the training sessions, and if you are fair with him, he is fair with you."

Kevin had his share of battles

'Bobby's the best' — Beattie

with Bobby over the years, but he still has a high regard for his former boss.

"You have arguments in every walk of life, but Bobby never held any grudges," says Kevin, who was capped nine times by England.

"He was like a father figure to me when I came down from Carlisle after leaving school.

"Ipswich were only just holding their own in the First Division when I arrived, but gradually he drafted in young players from his youth policy and transformed the club into one of the most consistent in the country.

"If you are good enough, no matter what your age, he will put you in the team.

"If he does take over the England job it will be a massive blow to Ipswich because he will be difficult to replace.

"The board of directors are shrewd enough to enlist Bobby's assistance in appointing a successor and it will be up to the players to keep producing the goods on the field."

Bobby Robson in pensive mood — England 'B' suffered only one defeat in 12 matches under his control and, in his 12 full seasons at Portman Road, Ipswich have finished outside the top six on only three occasions.

HEIR APPARENT

BOBBY ROBSON became number one contender for the England manager's job when he took charge of the England 'B' team in 1978.

In twelve 'B' internationals under his control, England won eight and lost only once — going down 3-2 in Spain in March last year.

ROBSON'S RECORD IN CHARGE OF ENGLAND 'B'

May 30, 1978:
Malaysia (1) 1 England 'B' (1) 1 (Kennedy A.).
June 7, 1978:
New Zealand (0) 0, England 'B' (2) 4 (Talbot, Needham, Hollins, Hill).
June 11, 1978:
New Zealand (0) 1, England 'B' (0) 3 (Anderson, Needham, Hill).
June 14, 1978:
New Zealand (0) 1, England 'B' (2) 4 (Talbot 2, Speight, Mariner).
June 18, 1978:
Singapore (0) 0, England 'B' (1) 8 (Anderson, Kennedy A., Daley, Mariner, Langley, Hill (2), Eves).
Nov. 28, 1978:
Czechoslovakia 'B' (0) 0,

England 'B' (0) 1 (Daley).
June 12, 1979:
Austria 'B' (0) 0, England 'B' (1) 1 (Robson) (abandoned after one hour — lightning).
May 31, 1980:
Australia (0) 1, England (2) 2 (Hoddle, Mariner).
Oct. 14, 1980:
England 'B' (0) 1 (Statham), USA (0) 0.
Nov. 17, 1980:
England 'B' (0) 1 (Sunderland), Australia (0) 0.
March 25, 1981:
Spain 'B' (2) 3, England 'B' (0) 2 (Statham, Martin).
June 2, 1982:
Iceland (1) 1, England XI (0) 1 (Goddard).

Robson ready to take England reins

IF Bobby Robson does become the next England manager then he will leave Ipswich with one major ambition unfulfilled . . . winning the League Championship.

But no other team in the country has gone closer without actually lifting the crown since Bobby took over at Portman Road in January 1969.

In 12 full seasons at the club, Ipswich have only been out of the top six on three occasions, and on one of those, they lifted the FA Cup for the first time.

They have been runners-up for the past two seasons and, in 1980-81, collected their first piece of European silverware — the UEFA Cup — on their sixth

Continental excursion.

But the title has somehow eluded Bobby, who was hoping to emulate one of his Ipswich, and perhaps England predecessors, Sir Alf Ramsey, who achieved it back in 1961-62.

IPSWICH TOWN'S LEAGUE RECORD UNDER ROBSON

Season	Division	Position
1969-70	1	18th
1970-71	1	19th
1971-72	1	13th
1972-73	1	4th
1973-74	1	4th
1974-75	1	3rd
1975-76	1	6th
1976-77	1	3rd
1977-78	1	18th
1978-79	1	6th
1979-80	1	3rd
1980-81	1	2nd
1981-82	1	2nd

White-shirted Bill Shankly in his playing days with Preston Here he challenges Arsenal's Doug Lishman at Highbury.

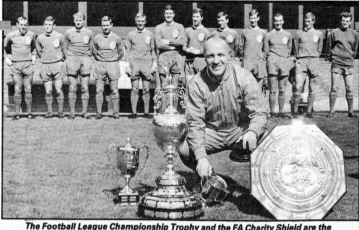

The Football League Championship Trophy and the FA Charity Shield are the centrepieces as Bill Shankly proudly poses with his great 1965-66 Liverpool side.

SHANKLY

MATCH WEEKLY'S tribute to the man who made Liverpool great . . .

...a Liverpool legend

FORMER Liverpool manager Bill Shankly was a legend in his own lifetime.

With his death at the age of 67, football has lost one of its most popular, wisest and most imitated characters. He was probably the greatest post-war manager.

The tough, straight-talking Scot moulded Liverpool into one of the most successful and feared club sides in the world, lifting them from the Second Division to win three Football League championships, two FA Cups and the UEFA Cup during his 15-year reign.

From that solid foundation, his successor, Bob Paisley, has taken Liverpool to even greater heights with three European Cup triumphs, but even he would be the first to admit that 'Shanks' was 'Mr Liverpool'.

In a tribute to his predecessor, Bob said: "Bill was one of the greatest managers there has ever been. I am deeply, deeply shocked.

And Tommy Smith, club skipper for five

'HE MUST NEVER BE FORGOTTEN'

years during Bill's reign, said: "I owe my career to him. He was a real fighter. He never knew how to lose."

The last word comes from former Liverpool player and now England captain, Kevin Keegan:

"I think I got as close as any player could to him and that's a real bonus.

"He was the sort of man you thought would never die and I just hope and pray now that Liverpool Football Club do something so that his name is always remembered.

"Bill Shankly must never be forgotten in that city."

England skipper Kevin Keegan shows his great mentor, Bill Shankly, the European Footballer of the Year trophy.

FOCUS ON IPSWICH STRIKER
PAUL MARINER

FULL NAME: Paul Mariner.
BIRTHPLACE/DATE: Bolton, May 22, 1953.
HEIGHT/WEIGHT: 5ft 1 1½ins/12st 2lbs.
MARRIED: Yes, to Ali.
CHILDREN: None.
CAR: Saab Turbo.
PREVIOUS CLUBS: Plymouth Argyle.
TRADE BEFORE TURNING PRO: Mechanical engineer (fitter).
CLUB NICKNAME: P.M. or 'Marers'.
WORST EVER INJURY: Stomach muscle tear.
FAVOURITE FOOTBALL LEAGUE PLAYER AND WHY: Terry McDermott — a great team player and goalscorer.
FAVOURITE FOREIGN PLAYER AND WHY: Gunter Netzer — a great passer of the ball and exciting to watch.
BEST ALL-TIME BRITISH TEAM: Shilton (Forest), Burley, Hunter, Beattie, Mills (all Ipswich) (Leeds), Charlton R., Edwards D., Best, Law (all Man. United), Lofthouse (Bolton).

ALL-TIME INTERNATIONAL XI: The West Germany side that won the European Championship in 1980.
FAVOURITE AWAY GROUND: White Hart Lane.
FAVOURITE FOREIGN STADIUM AT WHICH YOU HAVE PLAYED: Geoffroy Guichard Stadium (St Etienne).
BEST GOAL SCORED: Against Norway at Wembley in season 1980-81.
BEST GOAL SEEN SCORED: Terry McDermott's volley against Spurs in the Sixth Round of the FA Cup in 1980.
MOST DIFFICULT OPPONENT: David O'Leary of Arsenal.
MOST MEMORABLE MATCH: Ipswich Town's FA Cup final victory over Arsenal in 1978.
OWN MAGIC MOMENT IN FOOTBALL: England qualifying for the 1982 World Cup Finals.
BIGGEST DISAPPOINTMENT: Kevin Beattie's early retirement from football.

FAVOURITE OTHER SPORTS: Snooker, cricket, watching rugby.
MISCELLANEOUS LIKES: Rock music, Stan and Eddie of Coronation Street!
MISCELLANEOUS DISLIKES: Being late/smoking.
FAVOURITE TV SHOWS: Coronation Street, Porridge, Pot Black.
TV SHOW YOU ALWAYS SWITCH OFF: Top of the World.
FAVOURITE READING: Private Eye.
FAVOURITE POP STAR: Gillan, Saxon, Toni Basil.
FAVOURITE FOOD: Lamb and mushy peas.
FAVOURITE DRINK: Tartan bitter.
BEST COUNTRY VISITED: Italy.
FAVOURITE ACTOR/ACTRESS: James Cagney/Jacqueline Bissett.
BEST FILM SEEN IN PAST YEAR: Arthur.
BEST FRIEND: Johnny Wark.

BIGGEST INFLUENCE ON CAREER: Bobby Saxton — manager of Blackburn.
WHAT DON'T YOU LIKE ABOUT FOOTBALL: There's nothing I don't like.
SUPERSTITIONS: None.
PRE-MATCH MEAL: Grilled sole.
INTERNATIONAL HONOURS: Twenty-three full England caps.
PERSONAL AMBITION: To be healthy all my life.
PROFESSIONAL AMBITION: To win the League and League Cup.
CAREER AFTER PLAYING: Hopefully stay in football in some capacity.
PLAYER FOR THE FUTURE: Ipswich Town's Steve McCall.
WHO WOULD YOU MOST LIKE TO MEET: Ian Gillan and 'Biff' from Saxon.

1982-83

*Aberdeen, Rush & Dalglish
and Bob Paisley's farewell.*

1982-83

ROCKET MAN!

September 18, 1982

There's more quiz disc action with the chance to win a new VCR and meet Glenn Hoddle. Elton John hangs out with his Watford stars and the spotlight's on Sunderland starlet Barry Venison. Steak is his favourite pre-match meal.

LOTTA BOTTLE!

March 26, 1983

Steve Coppell prepares to play in his last ever final for Man. United before he's forced to retire with a knee injury. Sheffield Wednesday reach the FA Cup semi-finals and celebrate with pints of milk in the dressing room.

HELLO LINEKER!

May 7, 1983

Leicester hot-shot Gary Lineker appears on his first cover, seen here battling QPR's Bob Hazell as both sides won promotion. Inside, Gordon Strachan expects an Aberdeen shock in the Cup Winners' Cup final. They win 2-1.

RED DEVILS ROAR!

June 4, 1983

Man. United win the FA Cup replay, thrashing Brighton 4-0 five days after their 2-2 draw. Two-goal skipper Bryan Robson predicts United will go on to match arch-rivals Liverpool in all competitions. Sorry Brighton are relegated.

GOODBYE GLENN!

June 11, 1983

Glenn Hoddle tells MATCH why he's played his last game for Spurs, quitting White Hart Lane for a move to Italy, Spain or Germany. Four years later the Spurs midfielder finally packs his bags for Monaco, who play in France.

Kenny Dalglish

» STAR PLAYERS!

KENNY DALGLISH, Liverpool: An ever-present in the Liverpool team that led Division One from start to finish. Dalglish formed a deadly partnership with Ian Rush, bagging an incredible 50 goals between them.

IAN RUSH, Liverpool: Rush fired 30 goals for the second consecutive season, helping The Reds to the Division One title and a brilliant League Cup final win against deadly rivals Man. United.

Ian Rush

BEST KIT!

Man. United's Sharp home kit.

WORST KIT!

Arsenal's awful green away kit.

>> SEASON HIGHLIGHTS!

JULY: Ipswich manager Bobby Robson succeeds Ron Greenwood in the England hot-seat. Ron retires from football.

AUGUST: Kevin Keegan leaves Southampton and joins Newcastle for £100,000.

SEPTEMBER: Luther Blissett fires in four goals as Watford thrash Sunderland 8-0.

OCTOBER: England win UEFA's Under-21 tournament, holding off a West Germany comeback to win 5-4 on aggregate.

NOVEMBER: Former European Footballer Of The Year Allan Simonsen makes a shock £300,000 move from Barcelona to Charlton.

DECEMBER: England beat Luxembourg 9-0 with Luther Blissett grabbing a hat-trick on his first international start.

JANUARY: Spurs' Argentina star Ossie Ardiles returns to the club after his Falklands War-imposed loan spell at Paris Saint-Germain.

FEBRUARY: Liverpool beat Ipswich 1-0 to take a 15-point lead at the top of Division One.

MARCH: AFC Bournemouth enjoy a bumper crowd of 9,121 as fans flock to see the latest George Best comeback.

APRIL: Oxford chairman Robert Maxwell announces his intention to merge his club with Reading to form the 'Thames Valley Royals'.

MAY: Man. United's gifted 18-year-old Norman Whiteside becomes the youngest ever scorer in an FA Cup final.

Clockwise from top: Kevin Keegan and Peter Withe are axed from Bobby Robson's new-look England, Steve Foster with his headband, Bob Paisley wins the title in his last season as Liverpool boss and adds the Milk Cup to the Anfield trophy cabinet.

>> RISING STARS!

TONY COTTEE: Born just a few miles from Upton Park, the 17-year-old apprentice burst on to the scene after heading a goal on his debut against Tottenham in a 3-0 victory on New Year's Day. Cottee went on to bag an impressive five goals in just three starts that season.

NORMAN WHITESIDE: Man. United's Belfast-born teenager continued where he left off at the World Cup, missing just three league games all season and netting in the FA Cup semis and final.

>> FINAL LEAGUE TABLES!

DIVISION ONE

	CLUB	P	W	D	L	F	A	GD	Pts
1	Liverpool	42	24	10	8	87	37	+50	82
2	Watford	42	22	5	15	74	57	+17	71
3	Man. United	42	19	13	10	56	38	+18	70
4	Tottenham	42	20	9	13	65	50	+15	69
5	Nott'm Forest	42	20	9	13	62	50	+12	69
6	Aston Villa	42	21	5	16	62	50	+12	68
7	Everton	42	18	10	14	66	48	+18	64
8	West Ham	42	20	4	18	68	62	+6	64
9	Ipswich	42	15	13	14	64	50	+14	58
10	Arsenal	42	16	10	16	58	56	+2	58
11	West Brom	42	15	12	15	51	49	+2	57
12	Southampton	42	15	12	15	54	58	-4	57
13	Stoke	42	16	9	17	53	64	-11	57
14	Norwich	42	14	12	16	52	58	-6	54
15	Notts County	42	15	7	20	55	71	-16	52
16	Sunderland	42	12	14	16	48	61	-13	50
17	Birmingham	42	12	14	16	40	55	-15	50
18	Luton	42	14	7	21	65	84	-19	49
19	Coventry	42	13	9	20	48	59	-11	48
20	Man. City	42	13	8	21	47	70	-23	47
21	Swansea	42	10	11	21	51	69	-18	41
22	Brighton	42	9	13	20	38	67	-30	40

TOP SCORER: Luther Blissett Watford, 27 goals

DIVISION TWO

	CLUB	P	W	D	L	F	A	GD	Pts
1	QPR	42	26	7	9	77	36	+41	85
2	Wolves	42	20	15	7	68	44	+24	75
3	Leicester	42	20	10	12	72	44	+28	70
4	Fulham	42	20	9	13	64	47	+17	69
5	Newcastle	42	18	13	11	75	53	+22	67
6	Sheff. Wed.	42	16	15	11	60	47	+13	63
7	Oldham	42	14	19	9	64	47	+17	61
8	Leeds	42	13	21	8	51	46	+5	60
9	Shrewsbury	42	15	14	13	48	48	0	59
10	Barnsley	42	14	15	13	57	55	+2	57
11	Blackburn	42	15	12	15	58	58	0	57
12	Cambridge	42	13	12	17	42	60	-18	51
13	Derby	42	10	19	13	49	58	-9	49
14	Carlisle	42	12	12	18	68	70	-2	48
15	Crystal Palace	42	12	12	18	43	52	-9	48
16	Middlesbrough	42	11	15	16	46	67	-21	48
17	Charlton	42	13	9	20	63	86	-23	48
18	Chelsea	42	11	14	17	51	61	-10	47
19	Grimsby	42	12	11	19	70	70	-25	47
20	Rotherham	42	10	15	17	45	68	-23	45
21	Burnley	42	12	8	22	56	66	-10	44
22	Bolton	42	11	11	20	42	61	-19	44

TOP SCORER: Gary Lineker Leicester, 26 goals

DIVISION THREE

	CLUB	P	W	D	L	F	A	GD	Pts
1	Portsmouth	46	27	10	9	74	41	+33	91
2	Cardiff	46	25	11	10	76	50	+26	86
3	Huddersfield	46	23	13	10	84	49	+35	82
4	Newport	46	23	9	14	76	54	+22	78
5	Oxford	46	22	12	12	71	53	+18	78
6	Lincoln	46	23	7	16	77	51	+26	76
7	Bristol Rovers	46	22	9	15	84	58	+26	75
8	Plymouth	46	19	8	19	61	66	-5	65
9	Brentford	46	18	10	18	88	77	+11	64
10	Walsall	46	17	13	16	64	63	+1	64
11	Sheff. United	46	19	7	20	62	64	-2	64
12	Bradford	46	16	13	17	68	69	-1	61
13	Gillingham	46	16	13	17	58	59	-1	61
14	Bournemouth	46	16	13	17	59	68	-9	61
15	Southend	46	15	14	17	66	65	+1	59
16	Preston	46	15	13	18	60	69	-9	58
17	Millwall	46	14	13	19	64	77	-13	55
18	Wigan	46	15	9	22	60	72	-12	54
19	Exeter	46	14	12	20	81	104	-23	54
20	Orient	46	15	9	22	64	88	-24	54
21	Reading	46	12	17	17	64	79	-15	53
22	Wrexham	46	12	15	19	56	76	-20	51
23	Doncaster	46	9	11	26	57	97	-40	38
24	Chesterfield	46	8	13	25	43	68	-25	37

TOP SCORER: Kerry Dixon Reading, 26 goals

DIVISION FOUR

	CLUB	P	W	D	L	F	A	GD	Pts
1	Wimbledon	46	29	11	6	96	45	+51	98
2	Hull	46	25	15	6	75	34	+41	90
3	Port Vale	46	26	10	10	67	34	+33	88
4	Scunthorpe	46	23	14	9	71	42	+29	83
5	Bury	46	23	12	11	74	46	+28	81
6	Colchester	46	24	9	13	75	55	+20	81
7	York	46	22	13	11	88	58	+30	79
8	Swindon	46	19	11	16	61	54	+7	68
9	Peterborough	46	17	13	16	58	52	+6	64
10	Mansfield	46	16	13	17	61	70	-9	61
11	Halifax	46	16	12	18	59	66	-7	60
12	Torquay	46	17	7	22	56	65	-9	58
13	Chester	46	15	11	20	55	60	-5	56
14	Bristol City	46	13	17	16	59	70	-11	56
15	Northampton	46	14	12	20	65	75	-10	54
16	Stockport	46	14	12	20	60	79	-19	54
17	Darlington	46	13	13	20	61	71	-10	52
18	Aldershot	46	12	15	19	61	82	-21	51
19	Tranmere	46	13	11	22	49	71	-22	50
20	Rochdale	46	11	16	19	55	73	-18	49
21	Blackpool	46	13	12	21	55	74	-19	49
22	Hartlepool	46	13	9	24	46	76	-30	48
23	Crewe	46	11	8	27	53	71	-18	41
24	Hereford	46	8	27	42	79	-37	41

TOP SCORER: Steve Cammack Scunthorpe, 25 goals

'MY GEORDIE PRIDE'

BY KEVIN KEEGAN

ENGLAND'S best-loved player tells Match Weekly the inside story on the transfer sensation that rocked football.

MY TRANSFER to Newcastle United could be the move that keeps me in England for more than another season.

As I revealed exclusively in my last Match Weekly column I was pretty well resigned to going abroad in a year's time.

I had just returned from the World Cup and I have to admit I was at a low ebb. Missing England's games in Spain hit me harder than most people will ever know.

I needed a new challenge and I felt that playing in another country could provide it. I fancied France and I had the chance to play for a French club.

Germany, America and even Japan were very real possibilities.

But now I have found that challenge much closer to home — in the shape of the famous black and white striped shirt of Newcastle United.

The club and the people have made it very clear that they want me here and that gives me great pride.

Already my yearning to try my luck abroad for the second time in my career is waning. I have come under the spell of the passion that is unique to North East football and if I am successful at St. James' Park I would be happy to end my days here.

By successful, I mean winning promotion to the First Division this season — nothing less! I know we have a real chance of doing just that. Otherwise I would not have come here.

The crowd alone are worth two goals at home and one away. They're fantastic and I just can't wait to play for them against QPR on Saturday.

Playing in front of the Liverpool fans was an incredible experience but perhaps this is the only place in the world where that could be bettered.

Tyneside is a sleeping giant in football terms. The area has been deprived of success for years, but if Newcastle can change that then there is no end to the potential here.

I know my move from Southampton happened very quickly and a lot of people were taken by surprise. I shook hands on the transfer within half and hour of meeting manager Arthur Cox and club chairman Stan Seymour.

But there hasn't been a moment since I signed when I have entertained any second thoughts. There were no panic decisions. Everything felt right about the club and the people involved. The sick feeling that I brought back from Spain was suddenly replaced with the same excitement I felt when I went from Scunthorpe to Liverpool and then on to Hamburg.

I had the same intoxication when I joined Southampton two seasons ago and I never regretted the move.

The Saints were good to me and I enjoyed playing for the club and the fans. Lawrie McMenemy couldn't have been fairer with me, right up to the time of my leaving.

He sensed my heart was no longer in it and he realised I needed a new challenge to make me tick. That's the sort of person I am. I need new targets, I need to push myself to greater things. I can't sit down for an hour without getting restless.

At St James' Park it will be Wembley every Saturday. The place will be alive with excitement and expectancy. They'll be chanting my name and the pressure will be on me from the start. Hopefully it will bring the best out of me.

I look forward to living up here. My father was a Geordie who worked in the pits at Hetton-le-Hole and I feel a real affinity towards the people. I want to do well for them and repay the belief they have shown in me by buying season tickets as if they are going out of fashion.

People have questioned my decision to step down into the Second Division, particularly when it comes to playing for England. But it's not something that worries me.

At 31 I'm realistic enough to know that I could be among the players to go now that England have a new manager in Bobby Robson.

But I strongly believe that if a player is good enough he will be selected, regardless of age. So the onus is on me to prove I'm the good enough and I think I can do that in the Second Division — just as Trevor Brooking has done in the past.

The Second Division is at its strongest for years and all the hard games I can expect will hopefully keep me sharp and on top of my game.

Recognised First Division clubs like Leeds, Wolves and Middlesbrough will be desperate to go straight back up after taking the drop. Then there's the threat from Yorkshire clubs like Sheffield Wednesday, Barnsley and Rotherham.

In London, QPR have got to be a good bet and neighbours Chelsea are yearning for a return to their great times in the top flight.

I just hope Newcastle will be up there with them and that I can play my own part in bringing back the glory days to the North East.

● Kevin Keegan was talking to Melvyn Bagnall.

NEXT WEEK: What Keegan means to North East football ... special Match Weekly report.

John Trewick, Newcastle's £250,000 record signing from West Brom last year, has been joined by £100,000 Kevin Keegan at St James' Park.

KEVIN KEEGAN
Newcastle and England

match weekly

CUP FINAL 83
Replay

Brighton rocker! Bryan Robson starts United's first half goal spree as he hammers the ball between Tony Grealish (4) and Jimmy Case (7). Team-mates Ray Wilkins (right) and Alan Davies look on.

Thursday, May 26, 1983
FA CUP FINAL REPLAY

BRIGHTON (0) 0
Attendance: 92,000 (At Wembley)
Receipts: £640,000

MANCHESTER UNITED (3) 4
Robson 25,44, Whiteside 29, Muhren pen. 63

Brighton		Manchester United	
Moseley	7	Bailey	7
Gatting	7	Duxbury	7
Pearce	7	Albiston	8
Grealish	7	Wilkins	6
Foster	6	Moran	7
Stevens	7	McQueen	7
CASE	8	ROBSON	9
Howlett	6 (sub Ryan)	Muhren	7
Robinson	7	Stapleton	7
Smith	7	Whiteside	7
Smillie	6	Davies	8

Referee: A. Grey (Great Yarmouth)
Match Rating:****

MATCH
weekly

Vol. 4 No. 39

Editorial and Advertising:
Stirling House, Bretton, Peterborough PE3 8DJ.
Telephone: 0733-260333.
Publicity, Circulation and Back Issue Depts: Bretton Court, Bretton, Peterborough PE3 8DZ.
Telephone: 0733-264666.
Published by EMAP National Publications Ltd.
Printed by East Midland Litho Printers, Oundle Road, Peterborough.
© 1983 EMAP National Publications Ltd.

Editor: Melvyn Bagnall
News Editor: Paul Stratton
Reporters: Anthony Hawkswell
Melvyn Beck
David Smith
Design Editor: Philip Jarman

Production: Michael Weavers
Photographer: Philip Bagnall
Editorial Secretary: Jacquie Apthorpe
Advertising: Kieran Hamill
Publicity: Ian Templeton

Subscriptions: Match Weekly Subscription Dept, Competition House, Farndon Road, Market Harborough, Leics.
Subscription rates: Inland £29. Overseas — surface mail £30, air mail £36 (anywhere in Europe).
Registered as a newspaper with the Post Office.

WEMBLEY FACTS

	Brighton	Man. Utd
Corners for	4	6
Free-kicks against	9	13
Offsides against	5	3
Shots on target	4	9
Shots off target	5	5

Below: It's that man again...Bryan Robson (7) steals in for United's third goal a minute before half time.

ROBSON

UNITED'S two-goal hero Bryan Robson clutched his cherished FA Cup winners medal close to his chest and sent out a spine-chilling warning to the rest of the First Division.

The England skipper, inspirational and instrumental in the 4-0 hammering of Brighton, confidently predicts a return of the glory days at Old Trafford: "This win has given us confidence and belief in ourselves. Now we can go out and match Liverpool in all competitions," says Bryan.

"The first trophy is the hardest one to win and I've always been convinced that once we got over that hurdle, others would follow.

"In the replay we were all determined to make up for the disappointment of only drawing 2-2 in the first game. We wanted to do it for our great supporters."

For Bryan, the Cup success is his first honour in senior football and he admits: "It is a fantastic feeling. To score two goals made it even more special for me.

"The only thing I can compare it with is when England beat Hungary at Wembley 1-0 in 1979 to qualify for the World Cup Finals. The atmosphere and occasion was incredible that night too."

By his own high standards, the midfielder's performance in the first Wembley clash with Brighton was below par. He explains: "I was making runs into the box too early and the Brighton defenders were able to pick me up.

"Brighton tried to attack us more in the replay and that gave us more space. I don't think Steve Foster improved the back four because Steve Gatting and Gary Stevens were their best players on the Saturday.

"Our defenders, Gordon McQueen and Kevin Moran, played much better the second time and we were more patient in our build-up and more clinical in our finishing."

Arnold Muhren became the first Dutchman to play in an FA Cup Final and he fulfilled a five-year dream. He says: "Ever since coming to England with Ipswich, I've wanted to win this.

"And it feels even better than I thought it would. We won the UEFA Cup at Portman Road but it doesn't compare with this."

The midfield star knocked the final nail in the Brighton coffin with United's fourth goal from the penalty spot — his first ever spot kick in English football.

"Our regular penalty taker, Steve Coppell, couldn't play so the manager asked for volunteers. No-one came forward so I decided to take the job."

RUBS IT IN!

TWO-GOAL BRYAN SHOOTS DOWN THE SEAGULLS

Even though it took United 25 minutes to get into their stride, Arnold was never worried that they would lose the replay. He says: "We were always in command and, when the second goal went in, it was all over.

"But Brighton should be given a lot of credit. They never stopped battling and kept plugging away."

United manager Ron Atkinson was full of praise for his team's performance: "They were superb. We set out our stall to attack and win the game. That's exactly what we did.

"For the first 25 minutes, Brighton played better than they did on Saturday but once we got into our stride, I was confident that the Cup was ours."

Scottish striker Gordon Smith, whose dramatic miss in the dying seconds of extra-time on Saturday cost Brighton the Cup, says: "I don't think 4-0 was a fair reflection of the game.

"United got the breaks in front of goal and their finishing was lethal. From our point of view, the second and third goals were bad ones to give away. After that it was just a case of plugging away and trying to salvage something.

"Gary Bailey made a tremendous save from Jimmy Case when we were two-down. If he had scored we would have been right back in the reckoning.

"The pressure was always on us and when United are three goals up, people like Arnold Muhren, Ray Wilkins and Brian Robson look like the best players in the world.

"But I'm not too down. I'm thrilled to have played and scored in an FA Cup Final. It's been a great experience for me and a marvellous spectacle for the fans. We provided them with two very good football matches."

Jimmy Melia, the Brighton manager, has no complaints about the result. He says: "There's no doubt United deserved it. They were the better team. We had our chance to win it in the first game.

"But I'm proud of my Brighton team. They didn't let anyone down. If they had been six or seven goals down, they'd have still kept battling away.

Top: Teenager Norman Whiteside rises to score United's second goal. Brighton skipper Steve Foster (grounded) and Steve Gatting (2) can only watch in horror.
Above: Norman . . . you beauty! Bryan Robson (7), Frank Stapleton (9), and Alan Davies (11) rush in to congratulate scorer Norman Whiteside.

"Bryan Robson's first goal was tremendous. He made it out of nothing. I felt the big difference in the United performance was the form of him and Frank Stapleton. They combined so well in the replay."

Jimmy is also quick to heap praise on Gary Bailey. "His magnificent save from Jimmy Case turned the game. He made three great saves and it would have been an injustice if he'd been beaten.

"Obviously I'm disappointed we didn't win, but we achieved a great feat just to get to Wembley. If I'd have said in January that Brighton would get to the Final, people would have laughed at me."

● FIRST COLOUR PICTURES FROM THE FA CUP FINAL REPLAY — Pages 10 and 11.

DAZZLING

THE city of Aberdeen gave us a sensational welcome after our fabulous European Cup Winners' Cup victory in Gothenburg.

There were incredible scenes as our open-top bus inched its way through the crowds. Ecstatic fans were hanging from windows and cheering on the rooftops. The whole city was at a total standstill.

The short journey from the airport to Pittodrie took two hours and, when we arrived at the ground, it was packed to the rafters. I never knew so many people lived in Aberdeen.

The European Cup Winners' Cup was the one I wanted to win this season and I've savoured every minute of our success. I want to remember it for years to come.

And we won in style! We deserved the victory and should even have beaten Spanish legends Real Madrid by more goals.

We got off to a dream start when young Eric Black put us ahead after just six minutes. It could have been his second of the match because a few moments earlier, he'd hit the bar with a great shot.

Right: Teenager Eric Black gives Aberdeen a flying start by beating Augustin's despairing dive after just six minutes.'

Below: Willie Miller and his Aberdeen heroes celebrate the greatest moment in the club's history.

And there was only one spell when I thought we were in trouble. That was for about 20 minutes after Juanito had equalised from the penalty spot. We suffered an attack of nerves.

It was a silly goal to give away. Alex McLeish made a mistake — his only one of the game — and goalkeeper Jim Leighton couldn't reach his back-pass. There was no doubt it was a penalty.

My fear then was that they'd get a quick goal — it sometimes happens after a team has just levelled the scores. But they were content to knock the ball around at the back.

In the second half, we pushed Peter Weir into a more forward role and it was all Aberdeen from then on. Before the interval, he had been playing as if he was marking their full-back.

The chances came thick and fast for us and I had two good opportunities. The best was minutes before the end when I hit a shot high and wide.

Even though the chances weren't going in and extra-time loomed, we didn't panic — we kept plugging away and I was always confident we'd break them down.

Just before the end of normal time, Eric Black limped off with a recurrence of an ankle injury and John Hewitt came on. What a handy bloke he is to have on the sidelines!

John, who got the winner against Bayern in the Quarter-Final, repeated his trick with a splendid goal. Peter Weir released Mark McGhee and his cross was superbly headed home.

The atmosphere was incredible and our fans were going mad. It was important that we didn't get carried away and let it slip in the last nine minutes. Usually the final moments in a match like that tend to seem like hours.

Instead, they just flew past. I think that was because we were still attacking them.

There's no doubt in my mind that once extra-time came along, the Spaniards weren't interested in scoring. They just wanted to keep us out and take us to penalties.

We were much fitter than them. Towards the end, they just didn't seem to have it in them any more.

As we expected, Real Madrid were very physical and I thought our lads did tremendously well to stay calm. They tried to bait us. I was elbowed in the face and spat at by the same player.

But in the end we had the last laugh. When the final whistle went, the Cup was ours. It was a dream come true for me.

Unlike some of the other players, I didn't jump around and do silly things. I stood there and drank in the occasion and atmosphere.

After Willie Miller held the trophy aloft, it was time for the celebrations and congratulations. We got telegrams from both the Queen and Prime Minister Margaret Thatcher.

Now we've climbed that mountain, there's another peak to be reached on Saturday when we take on Rangers in the Scottish Cup Final.

And anyone who thinks we're going there just for the ride must be joking. There'll be 30,000 of our fans at Hampden and we'll be determined not to let them down.

Gordon Strachan

● Gordon Strachan was talking to Anthony Hawkswell.

DONS

RIGHT: It's all over and jubilant Alex Ferguson is carried to the Aberdeen fans on the capable shoulders of big Doug Rougvie.
BELOW: The moment of glory that all Aberdeen — and Britain — had waited for. Victorious skipper Willie Miller holds the trophy aloft.
BOTTOM: The winner! Madrid 'keeper Agustin is lost as Aberdeen substitute John Hewitt glides home Mark McGhee's cross nine minutes from the end.

1 GREAT NEW SERIES

WELCOME to the first of three great new series which begin in your favourite soccer magazine this week.

'My Team' is a super series where winning managers talk frankly about their teams with fascinating and often amusing player-by-player profiles.

Kicking off is Dave Bassett — manager of Fourth Division Champions Wimbledon.

'My Team' is a series you won't want to miss so place a regular order with your newsagent by filling in the order form opposite.

My Team
WIMBLEDON

By Dave Bassett

❝THE current squad at Wimbledon is the best-ever assembled at Plough Lane.

And next season I believe we've got a good chance of surviving in the Third Division. In the past we've tended to bounce between the two grades — so much so that I've often thought about approaching Otis, the lift manufacturers, for sponsorship.

Staying up has got to be our main objective because it's something we've never done before. On the last two occasions, we came straight back down again.

Two seasons ago, when we were last relegated, we fought an uphill battle from the start. I had the heart ripped out of my side through injuries and had to rely on kids and free transfer signings.

Myself and assistant manager Alan Gillett put in a lot of hard work last season and the players responded. I've been impressed with their determination and enthusiasm.

We started off very well, but fell away badly in November — just after I'd won the Bells Whisky Fourth Division Manager of the Month award.

We didn't win a game that month and went down 4-2 at home to Halifax — our worst performance of the season. I was desperately disappointed with my team after that game.

I felt their attitude was all wrong. They strolled around the pitch as if promotion was a certainty. They thought they'd arrived.

That defeat taught them a lesson. You can't take anything for granted in football.

One of the highspots of the season was our 1-0 win over fellow promotion chasers Swindon on Boxing Day. They were going well at the time and we showed great character to win at their place.

Overall, the lads have done me proud and I'm sure if they show the same attitude next season we won't have to worry.

Let me introduce them to you . . .❞

BASSETT'S

MATCH weekly
Special Offer £5

EACH WHILE STOCKS LAST

5

MOULDMASTER
Mitre
FOOTBALL

Send £5 (including P & P) to Match Weekly, Mitre Football Offer, Bretton Court, Bretton, Peterborough, PE3 8DZ, using the coupon below.

DAVE BEASANT: Nicknamed 'Lurch', because at 6ft 4ins he looks like the character out of The Addams Family! Dave is an extremely good athlete and he is quick, agile and very safe.

Quite a few top clubs have watched him and I once had an offer of £40,000 from Geoff Hurst when he was at Chelsea. At 24, he is still young for a 'keeper and has a lot more to learn.

GARY PETERS: My left-back and captain. I got him on a free from Fulham at the beginning of last season because I felt we needed experience in defence. He's a winner, very determined and leads by example.

The other lads call him 'Bosher' because he doesn't understand the word gentle. He never kicks the ball less than 40 yards!

BRIAN SPARROW: Since coming on loan from Arsenal, he's never been on a losing 'Dons' side. I'd like to sign him if his club don't want a fee.

He's ideally built for a full-back and is a good touch player. His brother John plays for Exeter.

MICK SMITH: Known as 'Locknut' because he's a bit tasty in the air. He cost me £12,500 from Lincoln four years ago. At six foot, he's a big, determined lad — the sort you'd want to be left with at Dunkirk!

STEVE HATTER: I had to raise a few bob this season to bring the centre-half from Fulham after an impressive loan spell here. He's good in the air, has a nice left foot and is a good passer of the ball.

He could improve his defending in one-against-one situations although that should come with experience.

STEVE GALLIERS: 'The Midget'. I sold him to Crystal Palace for £70,000 the season before last and bought him back for £15,000. He had an unhappy spell at Selhurst and his confidence took a knock. He played better in his first spell here.

But he's an all-action player who is very quick and sharp. I'd like him to score more goals. He has a tendency to shoot when he should pass and vice versa.

STEVE KETTERIDGE: The club's best player last

Cup happy. Wimbledon skipper Gary Peters with the Fourth Division trophy.

MY TEAM! Manager Dave Bassett with his championship winning team. Back row (left to right) — Steve Hatter, Paul Fishenden, Mick Smith, Dave Beasant (and Dave Bassett!), Wally Downes, Mark Morris, Stewart Evans. Front row — Gary Peters (captain), Brian Sparrow, Kevin Gage, Steve Galliers, Glyn Hodges, Dean Thomas, Steve Ketteridge.

ALL-SORTS

INTERVIEW: Anthony Hawkswell.
PICTURES: Philip Bagnall.

season . . . and to think I was going to give him a free transfer last year! In the end, I thought: 'Why should another club reap the benefit of all the hard work we've put into him.'

The 23-year-old midfielder works very hard and never stops running. He's known as 'Weed' because all the other players bash him up!

WALLY DOWNES: Known as 'Gob'. This man is a nutcase! He's always doing stupid things like letting down the car tyres of other players and nicking their gear. He once rang Dave Beasant pretending to be Bob Paisley and asked him if he was interested in playing for Liverpool.

Despite that, he's got lots of ability and had a good season even though he's been playing with a pelvic injury for the last 18 months.

STEWART EVANS: Scored 15 goals, but it should have been more. There's room for improvement from 'Bambi' who needs to be more of an extrovert.

I got him from Sheffield United on a free and the 22-year-old has settled in well and proved to be a willing worker. He's good in the air and reminds me of Watford's Ross Jenkins.

JOHN LESLIE: Our leading scorer, but I'd have given him a free last close season if his contract had been up. He had a

nightmare in the Third Division.

The 27-year-old is a born goalscorer and applied himself better last term. He's got the ability but he needs to be more determined.

GLYN HODGES: His disciplinary record the season before last left much to be desired — he clocked up a record 51 points! We had a long chat during the

Wally Downes — described by his manager as the nutcase in the Wimbledon side.

break and his attitude since has been excellent.

Glyn played for Wales Under 21s last year and has got talent, control and vision. He plays wide midfield and I've had battles with him in the past trying to get him to work harder at his game.

ALAN CORK: When he returned from 18 months' absence because of injury it was like having spent £40,000 on a new striker. He slotted in so well it was difficult to believe he'd been away. He got five goals in his first six games.

Everyone calls him 'Baldie' because of his lack of hair and kid him he's really 44 and not 24.

MARK MORRIS: Useful young reserve to have around. He can play centre-half, full-back and the odd time in midfield — if you're lucky!

'Guppy' — he goes around with his mouth open like the fish — is a real battler. He first came into the side when things weren't going well the season before last and proved his mettle.

KEVIN GAGE: England Youth international last year. He's very talented and has good control. He had a spell in the side before illness and eventually lost his place to Glyn Hodges.

Unfortunately, he cracked his ribs against Halifax, At 19 he's still learning the game and could prove a very good attacking midfield player in the next few years.

DEAN THOMAS: Cost me £8,000 from Nuneaton Borough and he's been worth the money. He can play

left-back or midfield. He's currently on duty in Finland after recovering from a cartilage injury. Because of his moustache everyone calls him 'Adolf'. The question is: 'Did he write those fake Hitler Diaries?'

● DON'T miss next week's 'Match' for a full colour picture of Wimbledon with the Fourth Division trophy.

Hans Van Breukelen

FULL NAME: Johannes Franciscus Van Breukelen.
BIRTHPLACE/DATE: Utrecht/October 4, 1956.
HEIGHT/WEIGHT: 6ft 2ins/13st
MARRIED: Yes, to Karen.
CAR: Fiat Strada.
PREVIOUS CLUB: FC Utrecht.
TRADE BEFORE TURNING PRO: Teacher.
NICKNAME AT THE CLUB AND WHY: 'The nose'.
WORST EVER INJURY: Cartilage injury this season.
FAVOURITE FOOTBALL LEAGUE PLAYER AND WHY: Ian
Bowyer. The Forest skipper always works hard for the team
and helps the younger players.
FAVOURITE OTHER TEAM: FC Utrecht.
FAVOURITE FOREIGN PLAYER AND WHY: Socrates of Brazil
— a great captain.
BEST BRITISH TEAM (current players): Shilton
(Southampton), Anderson, Todd (both Forest), Butcher
(Ipswich), Sansom (Arsenal), Coppell, Robson (Man. Utd),
Keegan (Newcastle), Robertson (Forest), Chamberlain
(Stoke), Mariner (Ipswich).
ALL-TIME INTERNATIONAL XI: Holland's 1974 World Cup
Final team with Jan Van Beveren in goal: Van Beveren,
Suurbier, Rijsbergen, Haan, Krol, Jansen, Van Hanegem,
Neeskens, Rep, Cruyff, Rensenbrink.
FAVOURITE AWAY GROUND: Anfield.
**FAVOURITE FOREIGN STADIUM AT WHICH YOU HAVE
PLAYED:** Volkspark Stadium (Hamburg).
BEST GOAL SEEN SCORED: Ian Wallace for Forest against
West Brom earlier this season.
MOST DIFFICULT OPPONENT: Every player who scores
against me!
MOST MEMORABLE MATCH: Winning my first cap for
Holland in 1980.
OWN MAGIC MOMENT IN FOOTBALL: Stopping a Luther
Blissett penalty in front of the Forest fans.
BIGGEST DISAPPOINTMENT: Losing to AZ Alkmaar in the
1982 Dutch Cup Final.
FAVOURITE OTHER SPORTS: Tennis, rugby, gymnastics.
MISCELLANEOUS LIKES: Playing for my country, winning,
good supporters and generally being happy.
MISCELLANEOUS DISLIKES: Wars, quarrelling and losing.
FAVOURITE TV SHOW: Sports programmes.
FAVOURITE READING: Sports magazines.
FAVOURITE POP STAR: Neil Diamond.
FAVOURITE FOOD: Pancakes.
FAVOURITE DRINK: Shandy.
BEST COUNTRY VISITED: Greece.
FAVOURITE ACTOR/ACTRESS: Jack Nicholson/Claudia
Cardinale.
BEST FILM SEEN IN PAST YEAR: 'One flew over the Cuckoo's
nest'.
BEST FRIEND: My wife, Karen.
BIGGEST INFLUENCE ON CAREER: Coaching staff at Utrecht.
WHAT DON'T YOU LIKE ABOUT FOOTBALL: Hooliganism and
bad referees.
SUPERSTITIONS: Some days I don't shave before a match.
PRE-MATCH MEAL: Steak.
INTERNATIONAL HONOURS: Nine caps for Holland.
PROFESSIONAL AMBITION: To be happy and healthy.
PROFESSIONAL AMBITION: To win something in the First
Division.
CAREER AFTER PLAYING: Teaching or training.
PLAYERS FOR THE FUTURE: Stephen Hodge and Colin Walsh.
WHO WOULD YOU MOST LIKE TO MEET: Princess Diana.
ADVICE TO YOUNGSTERS: Work hard and listen to advice.

*Princess Diana — accompanied here by Prince Andrew — is
the person Hans Van Breukelen would most like to meet.*

1983-84

John Barnes v Brazil,
Gary Lineker and Euro '84.

1983-84

CANNON ARRIVES!

August 27, 1983

MATCH celebrates the big kick-off with two perms on the cover, dropping 'Weekly' from the new logo and launching a Roy Of The Rovers-style comic strip starring Harry Cannon, illustrated by Man. City fan Steve McGarry.

STAR SECRETS!

December 24, 1983

Alex McLeish wants a Porsche for Christmas, Jimmy Case is off to see The Police and Simon Stainrod would love Rod Stewart to come round. Harry Cannon witnesses a fatal road accident near his club, Stanton Town.

MOST WANTED!

April 28, 1984

A MATCH special casts an eye over the English talent who could play in Italy. Bryan Robson is believed to have the best chance of success. Harry Cannon takes all his players to Benidorm for a mid-season break in the sunshine.

MARACANA MAGIC!

June 23, 1984

"It was the proudest day of my life," says England's John Barnes as he relives his staggering goal against Brazil on their own soil. Harry Cannon's Stanton snatch promotion from Division Four with a win over Tranmere.

MAGNIFIQUE!

July 7, 1984

Bryan Robson raves over French superstar Michel Platini, saying he's the world's best player as Les Bleus grab Euro '84 glory. Harry Cannon faces losing his star midfielder Nick Cannon on the eve of the Division Three campaign.

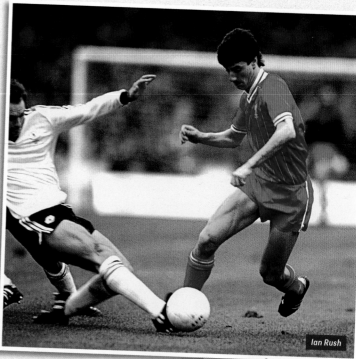

Ian Rush

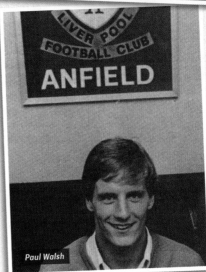

Paul Walsh

» STAR PLAYERS!

IAN RUSH, Liverpool: The young Welsh striker scored 47 goals as Liverpool again swept aside all challengers to win the league, the League Cup and the European Cup. At only 22 years old, the predatory striker was in top form, having scored 108 goals in three seasons.

PAUL WALSH, Luton: Before the long hair arrived, the penalty-box predator managed 14 goals for The Hatters, despite playing in a struggling side. Walsh ended the season by making his England debut on the summer tour of Australia – scoring on his second appearance – before making a £700,000 move to league winners Liverpool.

BEST KIT!

West Ham's home kit.

WORST KIT!

Chelsea's away kit.

54

>> SEASON HIGHLIGHTS!

JULY: Watford striker Luther Blissett makes a shock £1 million move to AC Milan.

AUGUST: Former England captain Bobby Moore becomes chief executive of Division Three side Southend.

SEPTEMBER: Tottenham become the first club to be listed on the London Stock Exchange and sell all 3.8 million shares at £1 within minutes of trading.

OCTOBER: Notts County lose their seventh consecutive league game in their local derby with Nottingham Forest.

NOVEMBER: England beat Luxembourg 4-0, but fail to qualify for Euro '84.

DECEMBER: Coventry beat Liverpool 4-0. Striker Terry Gibson hits the first hat-trick past The Reds in 11 years.

JANUARY: Division Three outfit Bournemouth beat Man. United 2-0 in the FA Cup.

FEBRUARY: Man. United turn down Sampdoria's offer of £2 million plus Trevor Francis and Liam Brady for Bryan Robson.

MARCH: Division Three Plymouth reach the FA Cup semi-finals, beating Derby 1-0 after a replay.

APRIL: Division Two basement boys Cambridge win for the first time in 32 matches by beating Newcastle 1-0.

MAY: England's Ray Wilkins joins AC Milan for £1.5 million.

JUNE: France win Euro '84, beating Spain 2-0 in Paris.

Clockwise from top: Live Sunday football comes to TV as Spurs play Nottingham Forest, Luther Blissett in his AC kit, Everton win the FA Cup final and Tottenham skipper Graham Roberts lifts the UEFA Cup with team-mate Gary Mabbutt after a tense final.

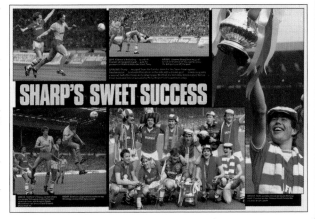

>> RISING STARS!

MARK WRIGHT: Southampton's rock-solid young centre-back was in fine form, guiding Lawrie McMenemy's Saints to a second-place finish, three points behind Liverpool, and earning an international call-up.

GARY LINEKER: Mark Wright wasn't the only new face in the England camp, as Bobby Robson was also impressed by Leicester's striker. Lineker made his Three Lions debut against Scotland in May 1984 after crashing home 22 goals for the newly-promoted Foxes.

>> FINAL LEAGUE TABLES!

DIVISION ONE

	CLUB	P	W	D	L	F	A	GD	Pts
1	Liverpool	42	22	14	6	73	32	+41	80
2	Southampton	42	22	11	9	66	38	+28	77
3	Nott'm Forest	42	22	8	12	76	45	+31	74
4	Man. United	42	20	14	8	71	41	+30	74
5	QPR	42	22	7	13	67	37	+30	73
6	Arsenal	42	18	9	15	74	60	+14	63
7	Everton	42	16	14	12	44	42	+2	62
8	Tottenham	42	17	10	15	64	65	-1	61
9	West Ham	42	17	9	16	60	55	+5	60
10	Aston Villa	42	17	9	16	59	61	-2	60
11	Watford	42	16	9	17	68	77	-9	57
12	Ipswich	42	15	8	19	55	57	-2	53
13	Sunderland	42	13	13	16	42	53	-11	52
14	Norwich	42	12	15	15	48	49	-1	51
15	Leicester	42	13	12	17	65	68	-3	51
16	Luton	42	14	9	19	53	66	-13	51
17	West Brom	42	14	9	19	48	62	-14	51
18	Stoke	42	13	11	18	44	63	-19	50
19	Coventry	42	13	11	18	57	77	-20	50
20	Birmingham	42	12	12	18	39	50	-11	48
21	Notts County	42	10	11	21	50	72	-22	41
22	Wolves	42	6	11	25	27	80	-53	29

TOP SCORER: Ian Rush *Liverpool, 32 goals*

DIVISION TWO

	CLUB	P	W	D	L	F	A	GD	Pts
1	Chelsea	42	25	13	4	90	40	+50	88
2	Sheff. Wed.	42	26	10	6	72	34	+38	88
3	Newcastle	42	24	8	10	85	53	+32	80
4	Man. City	42	20	10	12	66	48	+18	70
5	Grimsby	42	19	13	10	60	47	+13	70
6	Blackburn	42	17	16	9	57	46	+11	67
7	Carlisle	42	16	16	10	48	41	+7	64
8	Shrewsbury	42	17	10	15	49	53	-4	61
9	Brighton	42	17	9	16	69	60	+9	60
10	Leeds	42	16	12	14	55	56	-1	60
11	Fulham	42	15	12	15	60	53	+7	57
12	Huddersfield	42	14	15	13	56	49	+7	57
13	Charlton	42	16	9	17	53	64	-11	57
14	Barnsley	42	15	7	20	57	53	+4	52
15	Cardiff	42	15	6	21	53	66	-13	51
16	Portsmouth	42	14	7	21	73	64	+9	49
17	Middlesbrough	42	12	13	17	41	47	-6	49
18	Crystal Palace	42	12	11	19	42	52	-10	47
19	Oldham	42	13	8	21	47	73	-26	47
20	Derby	42	11	9	22	36	72	-36	42
21	Swansea	42	7	8	27	36	85	-49	29
22	Cambridge	42	4	12	26	28	77	-49	24

TOP SCORER: Kerry Dixon *Chelsea, 28 goals*

DIVISION THREE

	CLUB	P	W	D	L	F	A	GD	Pts
1	Oxford	46	28	11	7	91	50	+41	95
2	Wimbledon	46	26	9	11	97	76	+21	87
3	Sheff. United	46	24	11	11	86	53	+33	83
4	Hull	46	23	14	9	71	38	+33	83
5	Bristol Rovers	46	22	13	11	68	54	+14	79
6	Walsall	46	22	9	15	68	61	+7	75
7	Bradford	46	20	11	15	73	65	+8	71
8	Gillingham	46	20	10	16	74	69	+5	70
9	Millwall	46	18	13	15	71	65	+6	67
10	Bolton	46	18	10	18	56	60	-4	64
11	Orient	46	18	9	19	71	81	-10	63
12	Burnley	46	16	14	16	76	61	+15	62
13	Newport	46	16	14	16	58	75	-17	62
14	Lincoln	46	17	10	19	59	62	-3	61
15	Wigan	46	16	13	17	46	56	-10	61
16	Preston	46	15	11	20	66	66	0	56
17	Bournemouth	46	16	7	23	63	73	-10	55
18	Rotherham	46	15	9	22	57	64	-7	54
19	Plymouth	46	13	12	21	56	62	-6	51
20	Brentford	46	11	16	19	69	79	-10	49
21	Scunthorpe	46	9	19	18	54	73	-19	46
22	Southend	46	10	14	22	55	76	-21	44
23	Port Vale	46	11	10	25	51	83	-32	43
24	Exeter	46	6	15	25	50	84	-34	33

TOP SCORER: Keith Edwards *Sheffield United, 33 goals*

DIVISION FOUR

	CLUB	P	W	D	L	F	A	GD	Pts
1	York	46	31	8	7	96	39	+57	101
2	Doncaster	46	24	13	9	82	54	+28	85
3	Reading	46	22	16	8	84	56	+28	82
4	Bristol City	46	24	10	12	70	44	+26	82
5	Aldershot	46	22	9	15	76	69	+7	75
6	Blackpool	46	21	9	16	70	52	+18	72
7	Peterborough	46	18	14	14	72	48	+24	68
8	Colchester	46	17	16	13	69	53	+16	67
9	Torquay	46	18	13	15	59	64	-5	67
10	Tranmere	46	17	15	14	53	53	0	66
11	Hereford	46	16	15	15	54	53	+1	63
12	Stockport	46	17	11	18	60	64	-4	62
13	Chesterfield	46	15	15	16	59	61	-2	60
14	Darlington	46	17	8	21	49	50	-1	59
15	Bury	46	15	14	17	61	64	-3	59
16	Crewe	46	16	11	19	56	67	-11	59
17	Swindon	46	15	13	18	58	56	+2	58
18	Northampton	46	13	14	19	53	78	-25	53
19	Mansfield	46	13	10	23	66	70	-4	52
20	Wrexham	46	11	15	20	59	74	-15	48
21	Halifax	46	12	12	22	55	89	-34	48
22	Rochdale	46	11	13	22	52	80	-28	46
23	Hartlepool	46	10	10	26	47	85	-38	40
24	Chester	46	7	13	26	45	82	-37	34

TOP SCORER: Trevor Senior *Reading, 36 goals*

Above: Goal! With the Roma defence in tatters, stalwart defender Phil Neal (centre) repeats his feat of 1977 by scoring in a European Cup Final. Ian Rush (arms raised) celebrates Liverpool's 1-0 lead.

Below: All smiles and a handshake from striker Michael Robinson (left) and goalkeeper Bruce Grobbelaar as they parade the European Cup around the Olympic Stadium in Rome.

ERE'S NO PLACE LIKE ROME!

Above: What a team! Liverpool line up with the trophy.

Below: The scoreboard reads 3-3 but master marksman Ian Rush sends Roma goalkeeper Franco Tancredi the wrong way to put Liverpool 3-2 ahead on penalties and 4-3 ahead on the night.

Well done

We've won the Cup! The Liverpool team bus threads its way through the crowds — Steve Heighway, Emlyn Hughes, Bob Paisley, Bill Shankly and Kevin revelling in adulation.

KEEGAN MILESTONES

● Sept. 25, 1968 — Senior debut for Scunthorpe in 6-1 League Cup defeat by Arsenal.
● *May 3, 1971 — Joined Liverpool for £35,000.*
● Aug. 14, 1971 — Scored within minutes of his Liverpool debut in 3-1 home defeat of Forest.
● *Feb. 16, 1972 — Debut for England Under-23's in 2-2 draw with Scotland.*
● Nov. 15, 1972 — Debut for England in 1-0 win over Wales in Cardiff.
● *Jan. 17, 1973 — Wembley debut for England in 1-1 draw with Wales.*
● May 10, 1973 — Scored twice for Liverpool in UEFA Cup Final win.
● *Nov. 17, 1973 — Scored first League hat-trick against Ipswich.*
● May 4, 1974 — Scored two goals as Liverpool beat Newcastle 3-0 in FA Cup Final.
● *May 11, 1974 — Scored his first goal for England in 2-0 win over Wales in Cardiff.*
● March 24, 1976 — Skippered England for first time in 2-1 win over Wales in Wrexham.
● *April 28, 1976 — Scored in Liverpool's 3-2 win over Bruges at Anfield and then scored in the 1-1 second leg to help them win UEFA Cup for second time.*
● May 25, 1977 — Starred in his final game for Liverpool as they beat Borussia Moenchengladbach 3-1 to win European Cup for first time.

● *June 3, 1977 — Signed for Hamburg for £500,000.*
● July 26, 1977 — Scored for Hamburg on his debut in 6-0 friendly win over Barcelona.
● *Feb. 11, 1980 — Agreed to join Southampton at the end of the season for £400,000.*
● May 28, 1980 — Played in his second European Cup Final but Hamburg lost 1-0 to Nottingham Forest.
● *Aug. 19, 1982 — Shook football world by joining Second Division Newcastle for £100,000.*
● Aug. 28, 1982 — Scored winner on his Newcastle debut against Queen's Park Rangers at St James' Park.
● *Nov. 9, 1982 — Received OBE at Buckingham Palace.*

So proud in an England shirt and a popular captain.

KEEGAN FACT FILE

BORN: Doncaster, February 14, 1951
CAREER DETAILS:

Clubs	Lg apps	Lg goals	FA Cup apps	FA Cup goals	Milk/ League Cup apps	Milk League Cup goals
Scunthorpe	120	18	14	3	3	1
Liverpool	230	68	28	14	23	6
Hamburg			— not available —			
Southampton	68	37	5	2	3	1
Newcastle	76	46	3	0	4	1

INTERNATIONAL HONOURS: 63 full England caps and 21 goals; 5 Under-23 caps and 1 goal.

OTHER HONOURS: Three Football League Championships with Liverpool (1972-73, 1975-76, 1976-77). Bundesliga Championship with Hamburg (1978-79). European Cup winner's medal with Liverpool (1977). Two UEFA Cup winner's medals with Liverpool (1973 and 1976). FA Cup winner's medal with Liverpool (1974). Footballer of the Year (1976). West German 'Man of the Year' (1978). Twice European Footballer of the Year (1978 and 1979). English PFA Footballer of the Year (1982).

Kevin in action for German club SV Hamburg.

G' KEVIN!

UR tribute to Kevin Keegan —
soccer's best loved son — as he
es to bow out of soccer for the final

Farewell Liverpool. A wave to the Anfield faithful after playing his final game for the 'Reds' before leaving for Germany.

European Footballer of the Year for the second successive year, Kevin proudly shows the trophy to Bill Shankly.

Celebrating with the European Cup in Rome 1977.

In action for the first time in the colours of Southampton.

GOAL ONE! Spanish goalkeeper and skipper Luis Arconada fumbles Michel Platini's free-kick.

FANTASTIQUE

Vol. 5   No. 44

Editor: Melvyn Bagnall
News Editor: Paul Stratton
Reporters: Anthony Hawkswell, Melvyn Beck, David Smith
Photographer: Philip Bagnall
Design Editor: Philip Jarman
Production Editor: Michael Weavers
Editorial secretary: Jacquie Apthorpe
Ad manager: Terry Drudge
Ad secretary: Bridgette Pittam

Editorial and Advertising: Stirling House, Bretton, Peterborough PE3 8DJ. Tel: 0733 260333.
Publicity and Circulation: Bretton Court, Bretton, Peterborough PE3 8DZ. Tel: 0733 264666.
Printed by East Midland Litho Printers, Oundle Road, Peterborough.
© 1984 EMAP National Publications Ltd.
Subscriptions: Competition House, Farndon Road, Market Harborough, Leics. Rates: Inland £29. Overseas — surface mail £30, airmail £36 (anywhere in Europe).

Back issues can be supplied subject to availability at 60p each, including post and packing. Enquiries to Back Numbers Dept., Bretton Court, Bretton, Peterborough.

THE crown Michel Platini craved is his.

As the French skipper held the European Championship trophy aloft in glorious salute, he was finally acclaimed the best player in the world.

The dashing midfielder was the mastermind behind the breathtaking football that brought France their first major championship success.

And his incredible tally of nine goals in the Finals — a record for the Championship — left the watching world in no doubt that he is the number one.

Even the incomparable Brazilian master, Pele — the greatest player of all time — had to admit: "He's the best. Not only in Europe but better than anyone I have seen for years anywhere in the world."

Adds the great South American: "With Platini in the side, France are without doubt the top side in the world at the moment."

Pele is not alone in his admiration for the man who, despite not being at his brilliant best in the Final against Spain, could not help but make French history with the goal that set up victory for Michel Hidalgo's men.

Manager Hidalgo — filled with emotion after what was his last match in charge of the national side — said: "Platini has proved, with nine goals in five games, that he is the best in the World. There can be no doubt now."

Pele tells Platini 'You're the King'

After being chaired from the Parc des Princes pitch, he added: "It was a triumph for attacking football after years of defensive attitudes.

"I am delighted that the world has recognised the quality of our football and I feel honoured to have been the French manager."

Indeed, the Champions delighted throughout the tournament with thrilling victories over Belgium, Denmark, Yugoslavia and Portugal before facing shock side Spain in the Paris Final.

But it was drama to the death as the fluency of the French was threatened by the tough tactics of the stubborn Spaniards.

France took the lead with the softest of goals when Platini bent one of his famous free-kicks round the wall only to see poor Spanish skipper Luis Arconada — faultless in the earlier games — fumble the ball and allow it to trickle agonisingly over the line.

Arconada, his head in his hands, was inconsolable after his personal tragedy and Spain manager Miguel Munoz said: "We

all felt for him. Football has handed him a hard twist."

The veteran boss was furious at the decision of Czechoslovakian referee Vojtech Christov to give the free-kick in the first place.

He raged: "The foul was by the French player and it should have been our free-kick. It was a ridiculous decision.

"The referee clearly favoured France and we had no luck at all. I know they were the best team and deserved to win but remember we were without three key players and were playing them and their fans with a helpful referee in their own stadium.

"I'm happy overall, however, that we reached the Final and we now have a springboard for the World Cup in 1986."

Despite Spanish groans, it was the French who felt hard done by when sweeper Yvon Le Roux was sent off five minutes from time to set up a thrilling climax.

Said the dejected player: "When I was dismissed, I didn't feel it was right because I felt several Spaniards could also have gone during the game."

His team-mate Luis Fernandez leapt to the defence of Le Roux when he said: "He was unlucky to be dismissed. He made a fair tackle

● MICHEL THE MUSKETEER . . . special colour tribute on pages 20 and 21.

PLATINI'S PLEDGE:
'I'LL PROVE I'M THE BEST'

FRENCH skipper Michel Platini is out to claim the 'world's best player' tag in the heat of the European Championship Finals.

Speaking from the French squad's hideaway in the Pyrenees, the 29-year-old 'European Footballer of the Year' says: "I have been told that I am one of the best three players in the world along with Diego Maradona and Zico, but this is my opportunity to prove I am the best.

"I may lack their physical qualities, but I believe my form in Italy over the past two years will benefit me during the Finals.

"The two South Americans won't be on the home stage and there are few world players in the Finals.

. . . and that's what we encourage. I an see us scoring plenty of goals gain.

ntini picks out Yugoslavia and two other

team which is on the right running into form, not nimickable but with

Magnifique Michel! The world's best player — Michel Platini.

Robson raves over masterly Michel

BRYAN Robson — Britain's answer to Michel Platini — paid his own personal tribute to the French superstar when he said: "Without doubt, Michel is the number one in the world today. Since going to play in Italy, he has blossomed into a fantastic player."

Adds the Manchester United skipper: "He's such a good all-rounder. Everyone raves about his skill, but he also works very hard, tackles well and scores phenomenal goals.

"He has been an inspiration

for both club and country and ended the season with a glorious quartet of honours — European Footballer of the Year and winners' medals in the European Championship, Italian League and European Cup Winners Cup.

"It's almost impossible to beat such an incredible list of achievements."

Liverpool midfielder John Wark — himself a great goalscoring midfielder — is also lavish in his praise of the French skipper: "He has to be one of the best — if not the best — players in the world on his performances in the Finals. His nine goals alone say it all.

"I've been very impressed with the whole French team. Scotland played them just prior to the Finals and, although they beat us 2-0, it should have been more. I thought then that they would win the Championship.

"They have so many options and Platini has so many other players running for him."

● FULL results check from the European Championship Finals — Page 5.

FRANCE!

GOAL TWO! In the dying minutes of the Final, striker Bruno Bellone (11) chips Arconada after racing onto a pass from Jean Tigana to seal France's 2-0 victory.

— maybe a bit late — but it was at a time when the action was thick and fast so I think he was a victim of the atmosphere."

It came at a time when Spain were pressing hard for an equaliser but, despite the loss, it was ten-man France who aptly had the last word with an inspired second goal — typical of their exciting brand of football.

'Man of the match' Jean Tigana sent a superb ball through for Bruno Bellone to chase and the French striker sent a delightfully executed chip over the advancing Arconada to send the packed stadium wild with delight.

Bellone, tears of joy streaming down his face, said: "It's impossible to describe how I feel. After Platini's goal, we settled down a bit but were still nervous.

"It wasn't until I scored our second goal that we felt relaxed. I could see Arconada coming off his line and I knew I had to hit my shot absolutely right to beat him."

So it was left for the man himself, Michel Platini, to collect the coveted trophy and the Juventus ace summed up the feelings of all France when he said: "We have proved that France have the players and we may have been the best team in the world two years ago if we had been more experienced."

Of his own performances, Platini adds: "Before the competition, everyone talked about me, Maradona and Zico as the best three players in the world.

"Well, I finished top scorer in the Italian League and I've scored nine goals here. What else do I have to do to prove I'm the best?"

FULL NAME: Neville Southall.
BIRTHPLACE/DATE: Llandudno/ September 16, 1958.
HEIGHT/WEIGHT: 6ft 2ins/13st 7lbs.
MARRIED: Yes, to Eryl.
CHILDREN: None.
CAR: Datsun estate.
PREVIOUS CLUB: Bury.
TRADE BEFORE TURNING PRO: Hod carrier.
NICKNAME AT CLUB AND WHY: Jethro — because the lads reckon I look like one of the characters in the 'Beverley Hillbillies' — an old TV show.
WORST EVER INJURY: I've been lucky so far.
FAVOURITE FOOTBALL LEAGUE PLAYER AND WHY: Arsenal and Northern Ireland 'keeper Pat Jennings — he's so cool and calm.
FAVOURITE OTHER TEAM: West Ham.
FAVOURITE FOREIGN PLAYER AND WHY: Diego Maradona — a brilliant finisher.
BEST CURRENT BRITISH TEAM: Shilton (Southampton), Duxbury (Man. Utd), Hansen (Liverpool), Lawrenson (Liverpool), Bailey (Everton), Hoddle (Spurs), Souness (Liverpool), Robson (Man. Utd), Williams (Southampton), Rush (Liverpool), Dalglish (Liverpool).
CURRENT INTERNATIONAL XI: Shilton (England) and ten Brazilians!
FAVOURITE AWAY GROUND: Old Trafford.
FAVOURITE FOREIGN STADIUM AT WHICH YOU HAVE PLAYED: Bislet Stadium in Oslo.
BEST GOAL SCORED: Own goal v Watford (1982/83 season)!
BEST GOAL SEEN SCORED: By

STAR SPOT

Nev Southall leads the way with the FA Cup on the victory march following victory over Watford at Wembley last month.

SPOTLIGHT ON EVERTON'S FA CUP HERO...

NEVILLE SOUTHALL

Kenny Dalglish for Scotland against Belgium in the European Championship in 1983.
MOST DIFFICULT OPPONENT: Ian Rush.
MOST MEMORABLE MATCH: This season's Milk Cup Final and replay against Liverpool and the FA Cup Final victory against Watford.
OWN MAGIC MOMENT IN FOOTBALL: Collecting an FA Cup winners' medal.
BIGGEST DISAPPOINTMENT: Missing out on the European Championship Finals with Wales.
FAVOURITE OTHER SPORTS: I like watching most, but particularly American football.
MISCELLANEOUS LIKES: Walking the dogs and listening to music.
MISCELLANEOUS DISLIKES: Smoking and bad football commentators.
FAVOURITE TV SHOW: Minder.
TV SHOW YOU ALWAYS SWITCH OFF: 3-2-1 — it's absolute garbage.
FAVOURITE READING: Horror books and autobiographies.
FAVOURITE POP STAR: Dire Straits.
FAVOURITE FOOD: Chicken.
FAVOURITE DRINK: Tea.
BEST COUNTRY VISITED: Norway.
FAVOURITE ACTOR/ACTRESS: Sylvester Stallone/Bette Midler.
BEST FILM SEEN IN PAST YEAR: First Blood.
BEST FRIENDS: Brian Curran and his wife, Eileen.
BIGGEST INFLUENCES ON CAREER: My wife, my parents, Wilf McGuinness and Colin Harvey.
WHAT DON'T YOU LIKE ABOUT FOOTBALL: Losing.
SUPERSTITIONS: None.
PRE-MATCH MEAL: Chicken (when you can get it) but usually beans on toast.
INTERNATIONAL HONOURS: Fifteen full caps for Wales.
PERSONAL AMBITION: To play in the First Division until I'm 40.
PROFESSIONAL AMBITION: To win the League Championship with Everton.
CAREER AFTER PLAYING: I would like to own a farm.
PLAYERS FOR THE FUTURE: Ian Marshall and Micky Fielding — two youngsters at Everton.
WHO WOULD YOU MOST LIKE TO MEET: The person who pinched my watch at Oldham before the start of last season.
ADVICE TO YOUNGSTERS: Work hard and listen to good advice. Copy Everton full-back John Bailey — he's a model professional.

1984-85

*An FA Cup final red card, El Tel
and two football tragedies.*

1984-85

Peter Reid

CHIRPY CANARIES!

March 16, 1985

Mick Channon and Asa Hartford crack open the bubbly as Norwich reach the Milk Cup final. Steve Bruce heads the winner from a corner after missing the same move during the practice drill in training that morning.

MORAN SEES RED!

May 25, 1985

Three days after winning the European Cup Winners' Cup, Derek Mountfield admits crying in the Wembley dressing room as Everton lose the Cup Final. Norman Whiteside curls home United's winner after Kevin Moran is sent off.

SAFE HANDS!

June 1, 1985

England Under-21 keeper David Seaman says it's a 'dream come true' as the Birmingham new boy is promoted to Division One. It's quite a turnaround – he began the season at Fourth Division Peterborough before joining Blues.

YOUNG LIONS!

June 29, 1985

A new-look England crush West Germany 3-0 in a pre-World Cup tournament in Mexico as Bobby Robson brings Kerry Dixon and Gary Lineker into the side. Leicester star Lineker later reveals in MATCH that he's ready to quit Filbert Street.

UNITED'S NO.1!

July 27, 1985

MATCH turns the spotlight on Old Trafford's keepers, with the arrival of Chris Turner from Sunderland. The former Rokerite says he 'starts on equal terms' with Gary Bailey, but plays just 64 games before leaving three years later.

MARK HUGHES
MAN UTD & WALES

MATCH

» STAR PLAYERS!

PETER REID, Everton: The tough midfielder was an inspiration as Howard Kendall's side won a League and European Cup Winners' Cup double. A relative veteran at 29 years old, Reid made his England debut against Mexico in the summer of 1985, but was often used as back-up for captain Bryan Robson.

MARK HUGHES, Man. United: The 21-year-old striker netted 25 goals as his physical presence helped Ron Atkinson's United to fourth place in the league and success in the FA Cup. Earlier in the year, Hughes celebrated his international debut for Wales by netting the only goal of the game against England.

BEST KIT!

Nottingham Forest's SKOL kit.

WORST KIT!

West Brom's 'No Smoking' kit.

>> SEASON HIGHLIGHTS!

AUGUST: Luther Blissett rejoins Watford from AC Milan. The fee is £500,000, half what the Italians paid a year earlier.

SEPTEMBER: Billy Bonds makes his 700th West Ham appearance against Watford.

OCTOBER: Portsmouth's 22-year-old striker Mark Hateley scores twice as England beat Finland 5-0 in their first World Cup qualifier.

NOVEMBER: Everton top the Division One table for the first time in six years after a 3-0 win over Leicester.

DECEMBER: Stirling Albion's 20-0 win over Selkirk in the Scottish FA Cup first round is the biggest win in British football for 93 years.

JANUARY: Nottingham Forest boss Brian Clough celebrates ten years in charge of the club by ignoring a specially organised awards function and flies to Tenerife instead.

FEBRUARY: Liverpool beat York 7-0 in an FA Cup fifth round replay, with John Wark grabbing a hat-trick.

MARCH: A Mick Channon-inspired Norwich side beat Sunderland to lift the Milk Cup.

APRIL: Stoke's 5-0 defeat by Man. United signals the start of a ten-game losing streak that sees them relegated with a record low 17 points.

MAY: 56 people die in a fire at Bradford's Valley Parade and 39 fans lose their lives at the Heysel Stadium before the European Cup final.

Clockwise from top: Everton beat Anderlecht on penalties to win the Cup Winners' Cup, Gary Lineker dreams of a World Cup spot, England take West Germany apart in Mexico and Kevin Ratcliffe shows off his double trophy haul at Goodison Park.

>> RISING STARS!

CHRIS WADDLE: Newcastle's mullet man bagged 13 goals, including a hat-trick in a 5-5 draw at QPR. He was then handed his England debut against Ireland and started a healthy rivalry with John Barnes.

KERRY DIXON: Thanks to his strike partnership with David Speedie, Dixon scored 24 league goals as newly-promoted Chelsea finished a surprising sixth. His talent alerted Bobby Robson who named him in England's summer trip to Mexico, where he hit five goals in two games.

>> FINAL LEAGUE TABLES!

DIVISION ONE

	CLUB	P	W	D	L	F	A	GD	Pts
1	Everton	42	28	6	8	88	43	+45	90
2	Liverpool	42	22	11	9	68	35	+33	77
3	Tottenham	42	23	8	11	78	51	+27	77
4	Man. United	42	22	10	10	77	47	+30	76
5	Southampton	42	19	11	12	56	47	+9	68
6	Chelsea	42	18	12	12	63	48	+15	66
7	Arsenal	42	19	9	14	61	49	+12	66
8	Sheff. Wed.	42	17	14	11	58	45	+13	65
9	Nott'm Forest	42	19	7	16	56	48	+8	64
10	Aston Villa	42	15	11	16	60	60	0	56
11	Watford	42	14	13	15	81	71	+10	55
12	West Brom	42	16	7	19	58	62	-4	55
13	Luton	42	15	9	18	57	61	-4	54
14	Newcastle	42	13	13	16	55	70	-15	52
15	Leicester	42	15	6	21	65	73	-8	51
16	West Ham	42	13	12	17	51	68	-17	51
17	Ipswich	42	13	11	18	46	57	-11	50
18	Coventry	42	15	5	22	47	64	-17	50
19	QPR	42	13	11	18	53	72	-19	50
20	Norwich	42	13	10	19	46	64	-18	49
21	Sunderland	42	10	10	22	40	62	-22	40
22	Stoke	42	3	8	31	24	91	-67	17

TOP SCORER: Kerry Dixon Chelsea, 24 goals

DIVISION TWO

	CLUB	P	W	D	L	F	A	GD	Pts
1	Oxford	42	25	9	8	84	36	+48	84
2	Birmingham	42	25	7	10	59	33	+26	82
3	Man. City	42	21	11	10	66	40	+26	74
4	Portsmouth	42	20	14	8	69	50	+19	74
5	Blackburn	42	21	10	11	66	41	+25	73
6	Brighton	42	20	12	10	54	34	+20	72
7	Leeds	42	19	12	11	66	43	+23	69
8	Shrewsbury	42	18	11	13	66	53	+13	65
9	Fulham	42	19	8	15	68	64	+4	65
10	Grimsby	42	18	8	16	72	64	+8	62
11	Barnsley	42	14	16	12	42	42	0	58
12	Wimbledon	42	16	10	16	71	75	-4	58
13	Huddersfield	42	15	10	17	52	64	-12	55
14	Oldham	42	15	8	19	49	67	-18	53
15	Crystal Palace	42	12	12	18	46	65	-19	48
16	Carlisle	42	13	8	21	50	67	-17	47
17	Charlton	42	11	12	19	51	63	-12	45
18	Sheff. United	42	10	14	18	54	66	-12	44
19	Middlesbrough	42	10	10	22	41	57	-16	40
20	Notts County	42	10	7	25	45	73	-28	37
21	Cardiff	42	9	8	25	47	79	-32	35
22	Wolves	42	9	8	25	37	79	-42	33

TOP SCORER: John Aldridge Oxford, 30 goals

DIVISION THREE

	CLUB	P	W	D	L	F	A	GD	Pts
1	Bradford*	46	28	10	8	77	45	+32	94
2	Millwall	46	26	12	8	73	42	+31	90
3	Hull	46	25	12	9	78	49	+29	87
4	Gillingham	46	25	8	13	80	62	+18	83
5	Bristol City	46	24	9	13	74	47	+27	81
6	Bristol Rovers	46	21	12	13	66	48	+18	75
7	Derby	46	19	13	14	65	54	+11	70
8	York	46	20	9	17	70	57	+13	69
9	Reading	46	19	12	15	68	62	+6	69
10	Bournemouth	46	19	11	16	57	46	+11	68
11	Walsall	46	18	13	15	58	52	+6	67
12	Rotherham	46	18	11	17	55	55	0	65
13	Brentford	46	16	14	16	62	64	-2	62
14	Doncaster	46	17	8	21	72	74	-2	59
15	Plymouth	46	15	14	17	62	65	-3	59
16	Wigan	46	15	14	17	60	64	-4	59
17	Bolton	46	16	6	24	69	75	-6	54
18	Newport	46	13	13	20	55	67	-12	52
19	Lincoln*	46	11	18	17	50	51	-1	51
20	Swansea	46	12	11	23	53	80	-27	47
21	Burnley	46	11	13	22	60	73	-13	46
22	Orient	46	11	13	22	51	76	-25	46
23	Preston	46	13	7	26	51	100	-49	46
24	Cambridge	46	4	9	33	37	95	-58	21

TOP SCORER: Tommy Tynan Plymouth, 31 goals

*Includes one match abandoned at 0-0. Result stands.

DIVISION FOUR

	CLUB	P	W	D	L	F	A	GD	Pts
1	Chesterfield	46	26	13	7	64	35	+29	91
2	Blackpool	46	24	14	8	73	39	+34	86
3	Darlington	46	24	13	9	66	49	+17	85
4	Bury	46	24	12	10	76	50	+26	84
5	Hereford	46	22	11	13	65	47	+18	77
6	Tranmere	46	24	3	19	83	66	+17	75
7	Colchester	46	20	14	12	87	65	+22	74
8	Swindon	46	21	9	16	62	58	+4	72
9	Scunthorpe	46	19	14	13	83	62	+21	71
10	Crewe	46	18	12	16	65	69	-4	66
11	Peterborough	46	16	14	16	54	53	+1	62
12	Port Vale	46	14	18	14	61	59	+2	60
13	Aldershot	46	17	8	21	56	63	-7	59
14	Mansfield	46	13	18	15	41	38	+3	57
15	Wrexham	46	15	9	22	67	70	-3	54
16	Chester	46	15	9	22	60	72	-12	54
17	Rochdale	46	13	14	19	55	69	-14	53
18	Exeter	46	13	14	19	57	79	-22	53
19	Hartlepool	46	14	10	22	54	67	-13	52
20	Southend	46	13	11	22	58	83	-25	50
21	Halifax	46	15	5	26	42	69	-27	50
22	Stockport	46	13	8	25	58	79	-21	47
23	Northampton	46	14	5	27	53	74	-21	47
24	Torquay	46	9	14	23	38	63	-25	41

TOP SCORER: John Clayton Tranmere, 31 goals

65

MATCH

Vol. 6   No. 30

Editor:	Melvyn Bagnall
News Editor:	Paul Stratton
Reporters:	Anthony Hawkswell, David Smith
Photographer:	Philip Bagnall
Production Editor:	Michael Weavers
Editorial secretary:	Jacquie Apthorpe
Ad manager:	Terry Drudge
Ad secretary:	Bridgette Tan

Editorial and Advertising:
Stirling House, Bretton,
Peterborough PE3 8DJ. Tel: 0733
260333.
Marketing and Circulation:
Bretton Court, Bretton,
Peterborough PE3 8DZ. Tel: 0733
264666.
Typeset by Typefont Limited
Printed by East Midland Litho
Printers, Peterborough.
© 1985 EMAP Pursuit
Publishing.
Subscriptions: Competition
House, Farndon Road, Market
Harborough, Leics. Rates: UK
and Eire £30. Overseas — surface
mail £33, airmail £38.50
(anywhere in Europe).

Back issues can be supplied
subject to availability at £1.30
each, including post and
packing. Enquiries to Back
Numbers Dept., Bretton Court,
Bretton, Peterborough.

Registered at the Post Office
as a newspaper.

Adorned with favours from the fans, the delighted Norwich players go on their triumphant lap of honour after winning the Silver Jubilee Milk Cup Final 1-0.

ASA'S

WHILE jubilant manager Ken Brown toasted his Norwich glory boys, dejected counterpart Len Ashurst was left to ponder what might have been on a day when Sunderland's Milk Cup luck finally ran out.

After a charmed passage through to the Final, the Roker Park boss was loathe to admit: "The Milk Cup got one back on us today."

He was talking about Clive Walker's tragic penalty miss which could have put Sunderland back in the game but served only to hammer the final nail in their coffin.

He added: "We have had our fair share of luck during the competition — notably against

SUNDERLAND'S LUCK RUNS OUT

Watford and then against Chelsea when we were awarded two penalties in the first leg — but it deserted us when we needed it most.

"And it was ironic that Clive Walker, who has had a fantastic Milk Cup, should miss the all-important penalty.

"But I don't wish to take anything away from the players because to reach the Final alone was a marvellous achievement by my young side and hopefully we can use it as a springboard to greater things in the future."

While both managers experienced different emotions, they were united in their praise for the fabulous reaction of both sets of supporters who helped put the game down in history as the 'Friendly Final'.

Ken Brown echoed the thoughts of his Sunderland rival when he said: "They were absolutely marvellous today and I can't praise them highly enough.

"The reception Sunderland's fans gave our players on their lap of honour was top class."

The smile says it all ... Norwich have won the Milk Cup and manager Ken Brown enjoys the acclaim of the fans.

WEMBLEY FACTS

	Norwich	Sunderla
Corners for	4	6
Free-kicks against	19	15
Off-sides against	2	5
Shots on target	7	3
Shots off target	6	3
Headers off target	5	2
Goals	1	0

MOMENTS THAT MATTERED

AN exclusive guide to the moments that made the Final...

TWENTY SECONDS ... David Hodgson almost gets the Final off to a sensational start with the first attack of the game as he thunders a shot just over the Norwich bar after being put clear by Walker.

NINE MINUTES ... Norwich use the speed of winger Louie Donowa for the first time as he races past full-back Nick Pickering, only to see his cross headed over the bar by Mark Barham.

TWENTY-ONE MINUTES ... John Deehan goes close. Louie Donowa's cross is superbly headed back into the danger area by Mike Channon and 'Dixie' puts another header just over.

TWENTY-NINE MINUTES ... Norwich mount another dangerous attack and stand-in defender David Corner clears off the line — again from dangerman Deehan.

FORTY-FOUR MINUTES ... Clive Walker, freed by David Hodgson, is brought down just outside the box by Dutchman

Dennis Van Wyk and the former Chelsea man blazes the free-kick high over the bar.

FORTY-SIX MINUTES ... John Deehan robs David Corner near the corner flag and his cross finds Channon. The ball comes back off Gordon Chisholm to Asa Hartford. Goalkeeper Chris Turner looks to have Hartford's effort covered, but the ball is cruelly deflected into the net by the unlucky Chisholm and Norwich are one up.

FORTY-NINE MINUTES ... The 'Canaries'

fans have hardly stopped celebrating their goal when full-back Dennis Van Wyk handles in the penalty area and Salford referee Neil Midgley points to the spot. Agony for Sunderland's Clive Walker as his spot-kick hits the post.

SEVENTY-THREE MINUTES ... In a typical charge on goal, Steve Bruce storms in to blaze a terrific shot just over the Sunderland bar from a Barham corner.

EIGHTY-FOUR MINUTES ... Sunderland's non-stop defender Gary Bennett tests

the Norwich 'keeper Chris Woods with what was only the 'Rokerites' second serious effort on goal. His long-range volley is well held.

EIGHTY-FIVE MINUTES ... Mark Barham goes so close with a spectacular volley after a cross from the ever-alert John Deehan.

■ *MORE EXCLUSIVE COLOUR PICTURES FROM WEMBLEY —*
PAGES 20 and 21.

NORWICH City's first-ever Wembley goal was enough to send the cock-a-hoop 'Canaries' singing all the way back to Carrow Road with the Milk Cup.

And, fittingly, it was Asa Hartford — the first man to play for three different clubs in a League/Milk Cup Final — who supplied the shot which brought the only score of the game.

But ironically it was Sunderland's Clive Walker — the hero against his old club Chelsea in the Semi-Finals — who was the 'Friendly' Final villain when his penalty miss cost the Roker Park side their chance of glory ...

● REPORTING from Wembley: Anthony Hawkswell and David Smith. Pictures by Philip Bagnall and Lawrence Lustig.

MILK CUP FINAL '85

DIAMONDS!

Europe next for Hartford & Co.

NORWICH hero Asa Hartford capped up the glory of his club's finest hour and immediately set his sights on Europe.

Success in the Milk Cup automatically guarantees Norwich their first-ever sortie abroad and the former Scottish international admits: "I'd love to play in the UEFA Cup with the club next season."

The hero of the 'Canaries' dramatic victory over Sunderland adds: "My contract here finishes at the end of the season but I'd love to stay as long as I can.

"I was joking before the Final that I could be playing for the Canaries' in the Bernabeu Stadium against Spanish giants Real Madrid. Now that dream doesn't sound so daft!"

It was the former Scottish international's shot in the 46th minute which deflected off unlucky Sunderland defender Gordon Chisholm for the only goal of the game.

And the 33-year-old veteran says: "I'm not going to claim the goal. It took a lucky deflection.

"Goalscoring has never been one of my assets as a player so I'm not going to start worrying about hitting the back of the net now!"

The former Manchester City and West Brom star looked set for the soccer scrapheap before his move to Carrow Road at the beginning of

the season, and admits: "Winning the Milk Cup with Norwich is the most satisfying moment of my career."

The veteran of three Wembley Finals adds: "When I arrived back from America in the summer, none of the First or Second Division clubs wanted to know me.

"I could have joined a host of clubs lower down the League, but I held out in the hope that a club from the top flight would come in for me."

Man of the match Steve Bruce (24), a goalscoring hero in the Semi-Final against East Anglian rivals Ipswich, joked: "I suppose I'll have to have my passport renewed now!"

certainly be his Dad's last appearance at Wembley, the former England international sneaked him onto the bench for the match against Sunderland.

With a mischievous grin on his face, the Carrow Road character admitted: "I smuggled him in because it meant so much to me for him to be there.

"Norwich turned a blind eye — but that's the sort of caring club they are. I wouldn't have got away with it anywhere else.

"Towards the end, Michael was getting so keen that manager Ken Brown was thinking of bringing him on as substitute," joked Mike.

And as a very special memento of the occasion, Michael Channon has a very special souvenir — his Dad's Milk Cup winners' medal.

Said Mike: "My daughter Nikki has my FA Cup winners' medal which I got with Southampton — now my kids have one each."

Sunday, March 24
MILK CUP FINAL

NORWICH (0) 1	SUNDERLAND (0) 0
(Chisholm og 46)	
Att: 100,000 (at Wembley)	
NORWICH	**SUNDERLAND**
Woods 7	Turner 7
Haylock 7	Venison 8
Van Wyk 7	Pickering 7
* BRUCE 9	*BENNETT 9
Mendham 7	Chisholm 6
Watson 7	Corner 6
Barham 8	(sub Gayle 6)
Channon 8	Daniel 6
Deehan 8	Wallace 5
Hartford 7	Hodgson 7
Donowa 7	Berry 6
	Walker 6

Referee: N. Midgley (Salford)
Match Rating ★ ★ ★

■ EVERGREEN Mike Channon turned 'smuggler' before Sunday's Milk Cup Final.

Determined that his 10-year-old son Michael should have a bird's eye view of what will almost

Below: Disaster for Sunderland as Clive Walker (11) watches his penalty beat the outstretched Chris Woods only to hit the post.

WELCOME

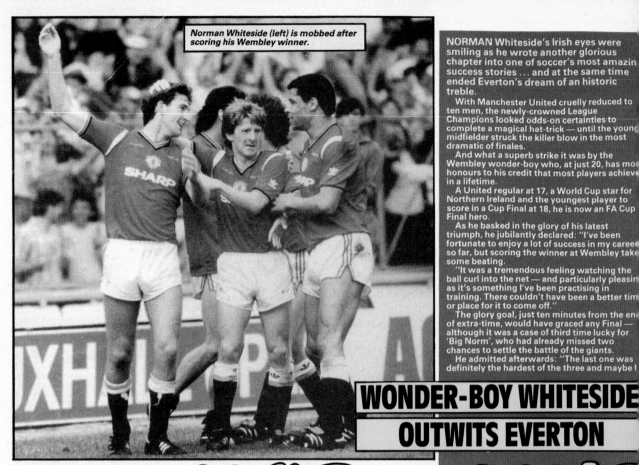

Norman Whiteside (left) is mobbed after scoring his Wembley winner.

NORMAN Whiteside's Irish eyes were smiling as he wrote another glorious chapter into one of soccer's most amazin success stories ... and at the same time ended Everton's dream of an historic treble.

With Manchester United cruelly reduced to ten men, the newly-crowned League Champions looked odds-on certainties to complete a magical hat-trick — until the young midfielder struck the killer blow in the most dramatic of finales.

And what a superb strike it was by the Wembley wonder-boy who, at just 20, has mor honours to his credit that most players achieve in a lifetime.

A United regular at 17, a World Cup star for Northern Ireland and the youngest player to score in a Cup Final at 18, he is now an FA Cup Final hero.

As he basked in the glory of his latest triumph, he jubilantly declared: "I've been fortunate to enjoy a lot of success in my career so far, but scoring the winner at Wembley take some beating.

"It was a tremendous feeling watching the ball curl into the net — and particularly pleasin as it's something I've been practising in training. There couldn't have been a better tim or place for it to come off."

The glory goal, just ten minutes from the end of extra-time, would have graced any Final — although it was a case of third time lucky for 'Big Norm', who had already missed two chances to settle the battle of the giants.

He admitted afterwards: "The last one was definitely the hardest of the three and maybe I

WONDER-BOY WHITESIDE
OUTWITS EVERTON

NORMAN'S

MATCH
Vol. 6 No. 38

Editor:	Melvyn Bagnall
News Editor:	Paul Stratton
Reporters:	Anthony Hawkswell, David Smith
Photographer:	Philip Bagnall
Production Editor:	Michael Weavers
Editorial secretary:	Jacquie Apthorpe
Ad manager:	Terry Drudge
Ad secretary:	Bridgette Tan

Editorial and Advertising: Stirling House, Bretton, Peterborough PE3 8DJ. Tel: 0733 260333.
Marketing and Circulation: Bretton Court, Bretton, Peterborough PE3 8DZ. Tel: 0733 264666.
Typeset by Typefont Limited Printed by East Midland Litho Printers, Peterborough.
© 1985 EMAP Pursuit Publishing.
Subscriptions: Competition House, Farndon Road, Market Harborough, Leics. Rates: UK and Eire £30. Overseas — surface mail £33, airmail £38.50 (anywhere in Europe).
Back issues can be supplied subject to availability at £1.30 each, including post and packing. Enquiries to Back Numbers Dept., Bretton Court, Bretton, Peterborough.
Registered at the Post Office as a newspaper.

CUP FURY! Manchester United skipper Bryan Robson (left) violently contests the sending-off decision which saw team-mate Kevin Moran (right) leave the field with 12 minutes of the match remaining.

should have made more of the other two opportunities.

"With the first one, Neville Southall made a superb save after I was put clean through, but the second one I made a complete hash of.

"Mark Hughes did some superb work down the left to pull the ball back for me, but I snatched at the chance and hardly made contact. The third more than made up for it, however."

And no-one was more relieved to see Norman's 110th-minute shot beat the seemingly impregnable Neville Southall and hi the Everton net than the unfortunate Kevin Moran.

The Eire international defender was reduced to tears when referee Peter Willis gave him his marching orders for a foul on midfield general Peter Reid.

He endured 30 minutes of torture on the United bench before Whiteside released him from his agony and he recalls: "I can't explain the relief and delight I felt when that went in."

About the controversial incident which led to him becoming the first player to be sent off in an FA Cup Final, Kevin said: "I just couldn't believe the referee's decision.

"There's no doubt that I went for the ball as Peter Reid came through, but I caught him when he pushed it away from me at the last minute.

"When the referee called me over, I thought he was just going to take my name.

"I began to walk away but he pulled me back and I was totally stunned when he pointed to the bench."

EVERTON'S HAT-TRICK BID ENDS IN TEARS

CUP FINAL FACTS

	MAN. UTD.	EVERTON
Corners for	3	4
Free kicks against	18	24
Off-sides against	7	9
Shots on target	8	4
Shots off target	8	4
Headers off target	0	2
Goals	1	0
Bookings	1	0
Sendings-off	1	0

FA CUP FINAL SPECIAL

● *Reporting from Wembley: Dave Smith.*
● *Pictures Philip Bagnall.*

EVERTON finally paid the penalty for their own success.

Two cup finals in the space of three days on top of a long, hard League season took its toll on Wembley's strength-sapping turf.

And, despite all they had achieved before — Champions of England and victorious in the European Cup Winners' Cup — it was still tears for souvenirs at Wembley as the magical treble was denied Howard Kendall's men.

Admits Derek Mountfield, so often Everton's Cup hero: "There was a feeling of total dejection in our dressing room. I was gutted and I don't mind admitting that I cried. A lot of the lads were in tears. We wanted that treble so much.

"When United had Kevin Moran sent off, we knew what we had to do but I think we were too tired to take advantage.

"We weren't able to up the tempo and, if anything, being down to ten men brought more fight from United.

"It was a very close game and both teams had chances to score but, in the end, I think United deserved to win. The winner from Norman Whiteside was a goal anyone would have been proud of.

"But we have still had a tremendous season. It was fantastic to win the League and victory in the Cup Winners' Cup in Rotterdam was an unbelievable occasion."

United defender John Gidman stretches out a leg to deflect a Peter Reid shot on to the post.

WISDOM
'We deserved it'
says Frank Stapleton

❝EVERTON have had a tremendous season, but Saturday was meant to be our day.

Their heavy commitments over the past few weeks seemed to take their toll on the League Champions and I think we wanted to win a little more than they did.

Even though we were down to ten men, we were definitely the stronger of the two sides and, in the closing stages, Everton looked dead on their feet.

We showed tremendous character following the harsh sending-off of Kevin Moran and when Norman hit the winner, it was no more than we deserved.

Everton can have no complaints and can't really argue that we were the better side on the day. But, ironically, it wasn't until we lost Kevin that we started to dominate.

At the start, both sides seemed very nervous and almost frightened to make a mistake. The first 45 minutes were spent feeling each other out.

It wasn't until the controversial sending-off that the game sparked into life and we started taking control. We began to create more chances than Everton.

We were so incensed by the decision and it made everyone left on the pitch give that little bit extra. And even when Norman hit that superb goal, we kept pushing forward and weren't content with sitting back on the lead.

In fact we had another couple of chances afterwards which really underlined our dominance during the latter stages.

We knew the main threat would come from the likes of Andy Gray and Graeme Sharp, but Kevin Moran and Paul McGrath did fantastic jobs in containing them.

And when the Eire defender was dismissed, the job of marking Andy was down to me. But I wasn't so much concerned about him as my positioning in a new role. I have played there once before, when Kevin was injured during the Milk Cup Final against Liverpool a couple of years ago, so it wasn't completely foreign.

In the end we got our just reward and it was a marvellous feeling when the final whistle went. It was great to present our fans with a much-needed trophy.❞

Right: Frank Stapleton celebrates with the Cup.

CAPTAIN DIEGO!

DIEGO Maradona is set to take over as skipper of Argentina.

Manager Carlos Bilardo has flown to Italy to talk with Napoli's £5million superstar about the prospect of taking over from former World Cup-winning skipper Daniel Passarella.

Bilardo maintains that 31-year-old Passarella still figures in his plans. He said: "It's just a case of a change for the sake of refreshing the outlook of the team."

But Passarella, who plays for Fiorentina and is regarded as one of the hardest defenders in the world, is reported to be unhappy with the switch.

BARCELONA GOES BERSERK!

Terry's the toast of Spain

Barcelona manager Terry Venables — "The greatest night in my football life."

AMID scenes of near hysteria, Terry Venables toasted "the greatest night of my football life" as Barcelona finally clinched their first Spanish Championship for 11 years.

More than one million frenzied fans packed the streets of Barcelona to welcome their heroes home following their 2-1 win over Real Valladolid.

And former QPR and Crystal Palace boss Terry said: "Nothing can ever equal this. We set out to do well from the start, but to win the title in my first season here is beyond my wildest dreams.

"The players deserve a lot of credit for the hard work they have put in this term."

And the man tipped to be England's next manager singled out former Tottenham striker Steve Archibald for special praise. He said: "Steve has done particularly well to blend in to a new team in a strange country. He has scored a lot of vital goals for us."

Barcelona made sure of the title they last won in the heyday of former Dutch World Cup star Johan Cruyff in dramatic fashion.

They needed a penalty save from their 'keeper Jabier Urruti just three minutes from time to secure the priceless two points.

Barcelona had opened the scoring in the eighth minute through Spanish international striker Francisco Clos but, within five minutes, the home side were level following a clever free-kick by Gonzales.

And the Barcelona fans had to wait until the 64th minute before they could start celebrating again when defender Jose Alesanco rose to head home a corner by Ramon Caldere.

From then on, until the final drama, the Catalan fans went berserk, setting off fireworks, waving their flags and dancing on the terraces.

The title success ensures Venables a huge pay increase and he is expected to sign a new deal worth a staggering £400,000 a year.

■ *VETERAN Chile striker Carlos Caszely celebrated his unexpected recall to big time international football with a two-goal burst for his country in their 6-2 World Cup qualifying win over Ecuador in a South American group match. The match was hit by a 13-minute black-out because of a power failure, but that did not stop Chile going top of their group.*

How they stand

FRANCE

	P	W	D	L	F	A	P
Bordeaux	29	21	5	3	58	20	47
Nantes	29	19	5	5	48	24	43
Auxerre	29	14	8	7	42	35	36
Toulon	29	15	5	9	35	28	35
Monaco	29	13	8	8	46	36	34
Metz	29	14	6	9	36	37	34
Brest	29	11	10	8	45	35	32
Lens	29	11	7	11	41	41	29
Sochaux	28	9	8	11	42	32	26
Paris St Germain	29	11	4	14	46	53	26
Bastia	29	10	6	13	33	52	26
Lille	29	8	9	12	31	33	25
Nancy	27	9	7	11	35	39	25
Marseilles	28	11	3	14	41	49	25
Laval	28	8	9	11	31	44	25
Toulouse	29	7	9	13	33	44	23
Strasbourg	27	7	8	12	34	40	22
Rouen	28	5	11	12	21	36	21
Tours	29	6	8	15	30	50	20
Racing Paris	27	6	4	17	22	47	16

LATEST RESULTS: Bordeaux 6, Auxerre 1; Nantes 1, Sochaux 1; Brest 3, Lens 2; Paris St Germain 1, Metz 2; Bastia 2, Tours 2; Monaco 3, Marseilles 0; Toulouse 1, Laval 1; Nancy 1, Strasbourg 1; Lille 2, Racing Paris 1; Toulon 1, Rouen 1.

HOLLAND

	P	W	D	L	F	A	P
Ajax	22	18	3	1	68	24	39
PSV Eindhoven	22	14	8	0	60	20	36
Feyenoord	21	15	3	3	64	30	33
Groningen	22	11	6	5	38	22	28
Sparta Rotterdam	22	9	6	7	33	41	24
FC Twente	21	8	8	5	36	36	24
Den Bosch	22	6	9	7	25	19	21
Utrecht	22	8	5	9	33	28	21
Roda JC	22	7	7	8	26	33	21
Maastricht	21	7	5	9	28	39	19
Haarlem	22	7	5	10	30	30	19
Volendam	22	7	5	10	27	42	19
Fortuna Sittard	21	7	4	10	23	30	18
Excelsior	22	4	8	10	24	34	16
AZ 67	22	4	8	10	32	43	16
Go Ahead Eagles	20	7	1	12	28	43	15
NAC Breda	22	4	6	14	19	37	12
PEC Zwolle	22	4	4	14	14	54	12

LATEST RESULTS: Fortuna Sittard 0, Ajax 2; Go Ahead Eagles 1, Sparta Rotterdam 2; AZ 67 1, NAC Breda 0; Den Bosch 0, Excelsior 0; Groningen 1, Maastricht 1; Utrecht 3, FC Twente 1; Feyenoord 6, PEC Zwolle 0; Roda JC 0, Haarlem 0; Volendam 0, PSV Eindhoven 5.

ITALY

	P	W	D	L	F	A	P
Verona	23	13	9	1	34	13	35
Torino	23	11	8	4	31	18	30
Inter Milan	23	9	12	2	27	17	30
Sampdoria	23	9	11	3	22	12	29
Juventus	23	9	10	4	37	24	28
AC Milan	23	8	8	7	25	23	24
Napoli	23	6	12	5	18	18	24
Roma	23	6	13	4	18	18	24
Fiorentina	23	5	11	7	26	26	21
Udinese	23	8	4	11	30	28	20
Atalanta	23	3	14	6	15	26	20
Avellino	23	5	9	9	15	23	19
Como	23	5	9	9	15	23	19
Ascoli	23	3	12	8	16	25	18
Lazio	23	2	10	12	12	33	14
Cremonese	23	2	5	16	14	37	9

LATEST RESULTS: Ascoli 2, Fiorentina 1; Atalanta 0, Udinese 1; Avellino 0, Napoli 1; Como 0, Sampdoria 0; Lazio 1, Roma 1; Juventus 3, Inter Milan 1; Torino 1, Verona 3, Cremonese 0.

SPAIN

	P	W	D	L	F	A	P
Barcelona	30	20	8	2	65	23	48
Atl. Madrid	29	15	9	5	47	26	39
Sporting Gijon	30	12	14	4	32	19	38
Ath. Bilbao	30	11	13	6	33	25	35
Real Madrid	30	12	10	8	43	30	34
Real Sociedad	30	10	11	9	38	28	31
Espanol	30	10	11	9	38	40	31
Santander	30	10	10	10	25	28	30
Seville	30	10	9	11	27	35	29
Valencia	30	8	12	10	36	36	28
Osasuna	29	11	6	12	33	33	28
Zaragoza	30	9	10	11	33	35	28
Valladolid	30	10	6	14	35	42	26
Malaga	30	7	12	11	20	32	26
Hercules	30	6	12	12	22	40	24
Real Betis	30	8	7	15	30	31	23
Elche	30	5	12	13	13	32	22
Murcia	30	5	10	15	20	46	20

LATEST RESULTS: Sporting Gijon 2, Malaga 0; Real Valladolid 1, Barcelona 3; Seville 2, Hercules 0; Santander 1, Atletico Madrid 2; Athletic Bilbao 3, Valencia 2; Zaragoza 1, Real Sociedad 2; Espanol 1, Osasuna 0; Real Madrid 5, Murcia 0; Elche 2, Real Betis 1.

WEST GERMANY

	P	W	D	L	F	A	P
Bayern Munich	24	14	6	4	52	32	34
Werder Bremen	23	12	8	3	65	37	32
Borussia Moen.	23	11	6	6	58	36	28
Bayer Uerdingen	23	11	5	7	46	34	27
Hamburg	22	9	8	5	40	31	26
Bochum	23	8	9	6	38	32	25
Waldhof Mannheim	23	9	7	7	34	37	25
Stuttgart	24	11	3	10	62	40	25
Cologne	23	11	2	10	45	43	24
Schalke	23	9	6	8	46	46	24
Eintracht Frankfurt	24	8	7	9	48	51	23
Kaiserslautern	22	6	9	7	27	39	21
Bayer Leverkusen	24	6	8	10	36	40	20
Fortuna Dusseldorf	23	6	7	10	39	44	19
Arminia Bielefeld	24	3	11	10	26	47	17
Borussia Dortmund	22	7	2	13	27	45	16
Eintracht Brunswick	23	7	2	14	32	50	16
Karlsruhe	23	3	8	12	31	62	14

LATEST RESULTS: Eintracht Frankfurt 1, Werder Bremen 3; Schalke 3, Arminia Bielefeld 0; Hamburg 5, Eintracht Brunswick 0; Borussia Moenchengladbach 7, Kaiserslautern 0; Stuttgart 3, Cologne 1; Waldhof Mannheim 0, Bayern Munich 0; Fortuna Dusseldorf 2, Bayer Uerdingen 2; Bayer Leverkusen 0, Borussia Dortmund 1; Bochum 5, Karlsruhe 2.

OTHER RESULTS

PORTUGAL: Farense 1, Porto 2; Setubal 2, Benfica 2; Guimaraes 1, Boavista 2; Academica 2, Rio Ave 1; Salgueiros 1, Braga 1; Penafiel 0, Belenenses 0; Varzim 1, Vizela 1; Sporting Lisbon 3, Portimonense 2. LEADING POSITIONS: 1 Porto 41 pts; 2 Sporting Lisbon 34; 3 Benfica 30. EAST GERMANY: East German Cup, Semi-Finals, First Leg: Dynamo Dresden 0, Vorwaerts Frankfurt 2; Dynamo Berlin 3, Magdeburg 4.

ITALY: Verona edged closer to their first ever Championship with a 3-0 win over bottom club Cremonese.

Three second half goals from Antonio Gennaro, Preben Elkjaer and Hans-Peter Briegel increased their lead at the top of the table to five points.

Meanwhile their nearest challengers, Inter Milan, slipped to a 3-1 defeat at European Cup Semi-Finalists Juventus. Sandro Altobelli shot Inter ahead, but the home side hit back through Marco Tardelli, Polish international Zbigniew Boniek and Massimo Briaschi, who finished off a superb Michel Platini-inspired move.

Inter's defeat allowed Torino to move into second place following a late winner by Austrian Walter Schachner in their 1-0 win over AC Milan.

WEST GERMANY: Werder Bremen sneaked closer to leaders Bayern Munich with an emphatic 3-1 win over Eintracht Frankfurt.

The second-placed side took full advantage of Bayern's 0-0 draw with Waldhof Mannheim to close the gap at the top to two points thanks to goals from Norbert Meier, Yasuhiko Okudera and the country's leading scorer, Rudi Voeller.

CYPRUS: Peter Cormack looks set to stay with his trouble-torn Anorthosis club after all.

Rocked by a bribery scandal involving four of his players, the former Liverpool and Nottingham Forest star threatened to quit following allegations that some of his stars had received money to 'throw' a game.

But an appeal from the rest of the squad has persuaded him to stay at least until the end of the season.

He says: "There are not too many games left this season so I have decided to hang on and try and win a place in Europe for the club. But I fully intend to return to Britain when the season ends."

FOOTBALL JOINS IN THE FUND-RAISING

ONE MAN who feels the tragedy more than most is Bradford City's player-manager Trevor Cherry, who has already auctioned off the Division Three Championship medal that was barely in his hand before the flames struck.

That raised £500 on BBC Television's 'Breakfast Time' and his pledge was joined by offers of gifts from many other soccer clubs. Leeds United, Cardiff, Coventry, Aston Villa and Spurs were among many others to offer items for an auction that raised thousands of pounds.

The whole fund-raising effort is being co-ordinated from Bradford itself, where the local council has set up the official disaster appeal.

Donations to the appeal can be made via banks to the National Westminster Account No 0178579783 or through the Post Office by using freepay 6009. Alternatively, donations can be sent direct to the Bradford Disaster Appeal, c/o Bradford Council, PO Box 85, Bradford, BD1 1HX.

Bradford City's players will also play their part. Several had friends and relatives injured in the blaze, while others had narrow escapes.

Captain Peter Jackson rushed into the stand where his wife Alison and young daughter Charlotte were watching. Alison jumped over a balcony, caught Charlotte as she was thrown down by Peter, who then jumped himself before leading his family to safety in a street adjoining the ground. He then returned to help shepherd people out of the path of the flames.

"It's really a terrible, terrible thing", he said afterwards. "To have started the day with celebrations and then to have it turn into this is almost too awful to talk about."

Cash is also pledged from many other charity matches, including the specially arranged clash between Chelsea and Glasgow Rangers, themselves no strangers to crowd tragedy after the 1971 disaster when 66 people died in a crowd stampede at Ibrox.

Right: Bradford captain Peter Jackson — rushed to the aid of his wife and daughter.

Safety first!

TAX CUTS NEEDED TO UP-DATE GROUNDS

Now is the time to act!

That's the united message from football in the wake of the fire tragedy at Bradford City that claimed over 50 lives.

It's the message from the clubs, the administrators and the fans who want to see the Government cut taxation on football betting and thereby release the necessary millions required to upgrade and make safe the shabby side of soccer.

And at the forefront of the Government's critics is the man at the helm of a club which has already shown the foresight and commitment to the causes of comfort and safety.

Fourth Division Chester City might not be everyone's idea of an ambitious club but, in 1979, they opened a brand new £650,000 stand that is the envy of many and a treat for their supporters.

It is costing the club between £25,000 and £30,000 a year to pay for and it is a burden they will have to carry for the next ten years.

But, says club secretary Albert Eckersley, it is a burden the club are happy to bear.

"I can say, without any fear of contradiction, that our ground will meet the required standards", he said.

"I dare say there are some who would say the money ought to be spent on the team but you can't please everybody".

It's also a burden that Mr Eckersley admits the club would be far better off without and casts the blame for that firmly in the Government's court.

"The Prime Minister has had plenty to say but what is needed is a cut in the taxation levied on soccer betting.

"We are not asking to be exempt, but we would like to be on a par with horse racing. They don't have to pay so much and so

The main stand at Chester — an expensive burden but a testament to the cause of comfort and safety.

consequently have been able to invest in some excellent facilities."

One man not so happy is Gordon Pearce, one of the best qualified men in Britain to talk about the comparative facilities at football grounds.

For Gordon is secretary of the 92 Club, the supporters who have visited all 92 grounds in the Football League.

He told MATCH: "The Government has got to take action. All they do at the moment is shout about the problem. The question eventually comes down to who pays the bill and I don't think that the amount of taxation on football is right. Not much of it comes back for the fan who paid the money in the first place."

One man not altogether in accord with the general view is Simon Inglis, author of the sell-out book 'The Football Grounds of England and Wales', about to be reprinted in a limpback edition.

"You cannot expect the Government to suddenly bail out clubs who have been mismanaging their affairs for a number of years.

"To be brutally frank, I think that some of the smaller clubs have shown how to go about their business while some of the others, in larger cities and towns and with larger support, have not.

"Having said that, I would say that there are about 25 grounds up and down the country where the design of stands is outdated and quite possibly dangerous, but the owners of those clubs are well aware of the dangers.

"I am sure there will be many developments during the close season but, as a guideline, I would add that I think nobody should be further alarmed. People shouldn't be afraid of going along to their local grounds."

MATCH SAYS...

THE horror is almost beyond belief. The sense of loss indescribable. The tragedy and despair of Bradford will live with us forever.

Harrowing though it was, television must be praised for bringing into every home the hideous scenes at Valley Parade. Only now are fans, club officials and Government bodies really aware of the dangers that could threaten inside grounds where safety measures have not been properly taken.

AND IT IS NOW THAT ACTION MUST BE TAKEN!

There has been much talk in the past of crowd safety. Hooliganism, too, has been the subject of specially commissioned reports. But not enough has been done.

Bradford came as a terrible reminder that talk is cheap. Ground tragedies and hooliganism are not new to the game. Action is what counts and it's at least encouraging to see the Government has announced plans to carry out safety checks at every sports ground and club in Britain.

The cost of improvements demanded by such a survey may threaten the very existence of some of the lower division clubs. If that is the case, then so be it. Nothing is more important than human safety.

MATCH extends its deepest sympathies to anyone connected with those people killed or injured in the Bradford disaster.

■ MATCH photographer Philip Bagnall attended the ill-fated game to take pictures of the Bradford team receiving the Third Division Championship trophy. His picture will now be used in next week's issue.

LIVERPOOL PAY THE PENALTY

BUT TRAGEDY OVERSHADOWS JUVENTUS WIN

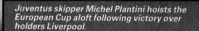

LIVERPOOL'S love affair with the European Cup finally came to a sad end in Brussels' Heysel Stadium as a Michel Platini penalty made it third time lucky for Italian Champions Juventus.

But it was a night overshadowed by an horrific pre-match tradgedy as fighting between rival fans caused a wall to collapse — killing more than 40 fans and injuring hundreds more.

The game itself started 85 minutes late and was reduced to a hollow occasion for injury-stricken Liverpool and their star-studded opponents.

Indeed it was a matter of some debate whether the match should have gone ahead at all, but the worried authorities were in a no-win situation whatever their decision.

In the end, it was all decided by a Michel Platini penalty after 56 minutes.

The super-talented Frenchman, who ran the show in the first half, produced an incredible through-ball for Zbigniew Boniek to chase.

And as Juventus' Polish striker bore down on goal, he was tripped by Liverpool's substitute defender Gary Gillespie on for the injured Mark Lawrenson who dislocated his right shoulder with his first tackle.

The TV cameras clearly showed Boniek was outside the box when he fell but there were few, if any, complaints from any Liverpool players. It was not a night for controversy on the pitch.

Up stepped Platini and sent Bruce Grobbelaar the wrong way to score with a crisply-hit drive to the keeper's right and so clinch Juventus' first victory in the competition in what was their third Final appearance.

Liverpool had all the possession in the second half but were unable to penetrate the Juventus defence. Maybe their hearts couldn't have been solely on the game.

Gary Gillespie — it was his trip on Boniek which led to the match-winning penalty.

Juventus skipper Michel Plantini hoists the European Cup aloft following victory over holders Liverpool.

So they became only the third British team to lose in a European Cup Final — Celtic in 1970 and Leeds in 1975 the only other two to return empty-handed.

Celtic, Britain's first winners of the trophy back in 1967, lost out to Dutch aces Feyenoord in extra-time while Leeds went down 2-0 to the powerful Bayern Munich side of the early seventies.

Indeed, since Liverpool landed their first success against Borussia Moenchengladbach in 1977, the coveted trophy has only been away from these shores on one other occasion — ironically when Hamburg toppled Juventus 1-0 in 1983.

This year's Final was the eighth in the last nine years with English interest and all the previous seven had ended with the Union Jack flying proudly in salute of victory.

Britain's record in European Cup Final appearances:
1967 (Lisbon) Celtic 2 (Gemmell, Chalmers), Inter-Milan 1 (Mazzola pen)
1968 (Wembley) Man. United 4 (Charlton 2, Best, Kidd), Benfica 1 (Graca) aet
1970 (Milan) Feyenoord 2 (Israel, Kindvall), Celtic 1 (Gemmell) aet
1975 (Paris) Bayern Munich 2 (Roth, Muller), Leeds 0
1977 (Rome) Liverpool 3 (McDermott, Smith, Neal pen), Borussia Moen. 1 (Simonsen)
1978 (Wembley) Liverpool 1 (Dalglish), Bruges 0
1979 (Munich) Nott'm Forest 1 (Francis), Malmo 0
1980 (Madrid) Nott'm Forest 1 (Robertson), Hamburg 0
1981 (Paris) Liverpool 1 (Kennedy A), Real Madrid 0
1982 (Rotterdam) Aston Villa 1 (Withe), Bayern Munich 0
1984 (Rome) Liverpool 1 (Neal), AS Roma 1 (Pruzzo) aet — Liverpool won 4-2 on penalties
1985 (Brussels) Juventus 1 (Platini), Liverpool 0

Sadly, due to the mindless behaviour of a section of fans, that flag has been well and truly trodden in the dust.

And as soccer awaited the decision of UEFA on the violence that caused one of the most horrific tragedies soccer has known, everyone feared the worst for Britain's future involvement in European soccer.

● FOLLOWING the tragedy in Brussels, MATCH will not be carrying colour posters from the European Cup Final.

OLD warhorse Mick Channon claims European competition will count for nothing without the involvement of English clubs.

But Norwich star Mick, one of a host of players whose European hopes have been blitzed by UEFA's decision, is adamant that the ban had to stand.

"Let's face it, without English clubs there is no European soccer!

"You've only got to look at the success of home clubs in Europe over recent years to realise that without us, the competitions will mean nothing.

"But I'm afraid UEFA had no alternative. Those were not real Liverpool fans we saw causing trouble in Brussels and who is to say that the same sick minority would not tag onto Norwich or Southampton fans if they were playing abroad?

"Obviously it's a real sickener for Norwich but now it's up to us to put things right."

As a boy, Southampton midfield star Jimmy Case used to cheer on his beloved Liverpool from the Kop and he says: "In those days, if a few kids got out of line they got a clip around the ear from the older fans, but now youngsters go to matches looking for trouble.

"I was looking forward to playing in Europe again after such a long break, but this means I will never get the chance.

CLUBS AFFECTED BY THE BAN

European Cup
EVERTON

Cup Winners' Cup
MANCHESTER UNITED

UEFA Cup
LIVERPOOL, NORWICH, SOUTHAMPTON, TOTTENHAM

"I feel sorry for the young players in our side. At least I've played in big European games. Because of this ban, they will probably never get the chance."

Liverpool skipper Phil Neal was so sickened by the Heysel Stadium scenes that he could not bring himself to discuss the UEFA ban.

All he would say was: "I'm blitzed. I'm still in mourning after what happened in Brussels. I've got so many happy memories from football but this was terrible."

His Liverpool team-mate Mark Lawrenson was more forthcoming: "I think the ban was

Right: Derek Mountfield — fears.

Below: Mick Channon — sickened.

BANNED!

IN an unprecedented move by UEFA following the crowd violence which marred this year's European Cup Final in Brussels' Heysel Stadium, English clubs have been banned from playing in Europe for an indefinite period. MATCH brings you the sad verdicts of the stars immediately affected as they come to terms with the devastating decision.

Left: Mark Lawrenson — staggered.

Above: Jimmy Case — sorry.

Above: Arthur Albiston — stunned.

to be expected but, after seeing the Juventus fans, I think the Italians should have been punished as well."

Claims the Eire international: "When the Liverpool fans had quietened down, the Italians were still causing trouble, but nothing has been said about that."

Mark admits he was staggered by the Belgian crowd control in the Heysel Stadium.

"I understand we had contacted them about crowd segregation but nothing seemed to have been done. It's terrible that after 21 years in Europe, it should all end this way."

Everton's Derek Mountfield was looking forward to his side's first venture in the European Cup for 15 years, but now he fears the ban has ended his European soccer career.

"I think UEFA did what they had to do, but this could go on for ten years. I doubt whether I'll play in Europe again," he says.

Everton are another club hit particularly hard by the ban. During their successful Cup-Winners' Cup campaign last season, none of their fans caused trouble, but Derek claims all English clubs have to take responsibility for the Brussels riot.

"Now is not the time to start pointing the finger at other clubs because we are all, in some part, responsible for the trouble in Belgium.

"Now is the time to get together and try and work out a solution before it is too late."

Arthur Albiston and his Manchester United team-mates were on tour in the West Indies at the time of the riot, but he was stunned by news pictures they saw when they arrived home.

They too have seen their Cup-Winners' Cup ambitions wrecked by the UEFA ban, but Arthur says they must accept the decision.

"This has been coming for a long time," he says. "For several years now, teams have been going abroad and causing trouble and I think UEFA have said 'enough is enough'. You can't really blame them can you?"

■ WHILE English clubs have been made to suffer for the Brussels outrage, Scottish, Welsh and Irish clubs escaped punishment and, over the page, we spotlight the mighty minnows of Bangor City who will be staging their European adventure in the Cup-Winners Cup next season.

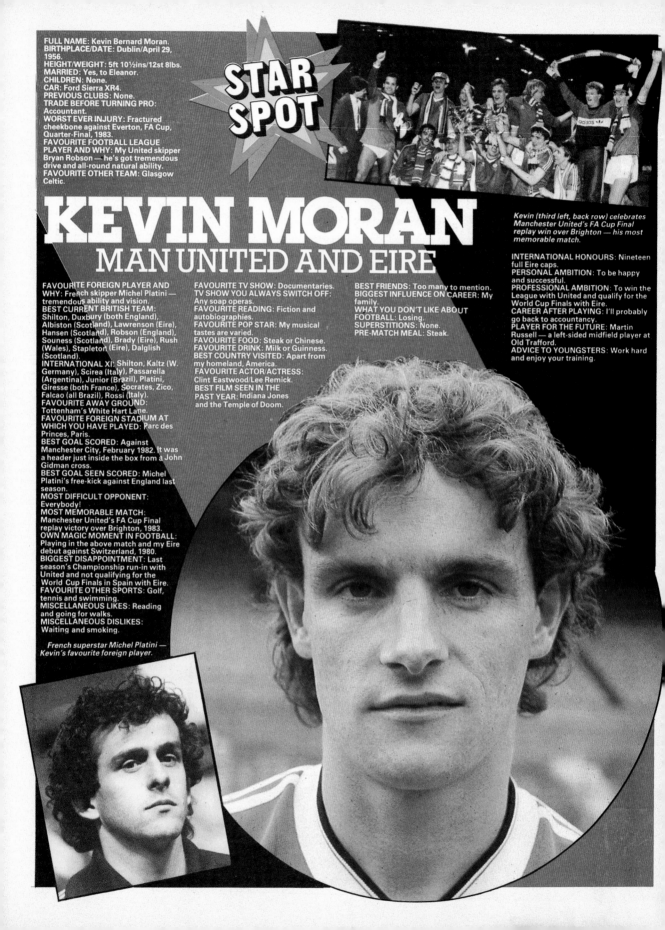

FULL NAME: Kevin Bernard Moran.
BIRTHPLACE/DATE: Dublin/April 29, 1956.
HEIGHT/WEIGHT: 5ft 10½ins/12st 8lbs.
MARRIED: Yes, to Eleanor.
CHILDREN: None.
CAR: Ford Sierra XR4.
PREVIOUS CLUBS: None.
TRADE BEFORE TURNING PRO: Accountant.
WORST EVER INJURY: Fractured cheekbone against Everton, FA Cup, Quarter-Final, 1983.
FAVOURITE FOOTBALL LEAGUE PLAYER AND WHY: My United skipper Bryan Robson — he's got tremendous drive and all-round natural ability.
FAVOURITE OTHER TEAM: Glasgow Celtic.

STAR SPOT

KEVIN MORAN
MAN UNITED AND EIRE

Kevin (third left, back row) celebrates Manchester United's FA Cup Final replay win over Brighton — his most memorable match.

FAVOURITE FOREIGN PLAYER AND WHY: French skipper Michel Platini — tremendous ability and vision.
BEST CURRENT BRITISH TEAM: Shilton, Duxbury (both England), Albiston (Scotland), Lawrenson (Eire), Hansen (Scotland), Robson (England), Souness (Scotland), Brady (Eire), Rush (Wales), Stapleton (Eire), Dalglish (Scotland).
INTERNATIONAL XI: Shilton, Kaltz (W. Germany), Scirea (Italy), Passarella (Argentina), Junior (Brazil), Platini, Giresse (both France), Socrates, Zico, Falcao (all Brazil), Rossi (Italy).
FAVOURITE AWAY GROUND: Tottenham's White Hart Lane.
FAVOURITE FOREIGN STADIUM AT WHICH YOU HAVE PLAYED: Parc des Princes, Paris.
BEST GOAL SCORED: Against Manchester City, February 1982. It was a header just inside the box from a John Gidman cross.
BEST GOAL SEEN SCORED: Michel Platini's free-kick against England last season.
MOST DIFFICULT OPPONENT: Everybody!
MOST MEMORABLE MATCH: Manchester United's FA Cup Final replay victory over Brighton, 1983.
OWN MAGIC MOMENT IN FOOTBALL: Playing in the above match and my Eire debut against Switzerland, 1980.
BIGGEST DISAPPOINTMENT: Last season's Championship run-in with United and not qualifying for the World Cup Finals in Spain with Eire.
FAVOURITE OTHER SPORTS: Golf, tennis and swimming.
MISCELLANEOUS LIKES: Reading and going for walks.
MISCELLANEOUS DISLIKES: Waiting and smoking.

French superstar Michel Platini — Kevin's favourite foreign player.

FAVOURITE TV SHOW: Documentaries.
TV SHOW YOU ALWAYS SWITCH OFF: Any soap operas.
FAVOURITE READING: Fiction and autobiographies.
FAVOURITE POP STAR: My musical tastes are varied.
FAVOURITE FOOD: Steak or Chinese.
FAVOURITE DRINK: Milk or Guinness.
BEST COUNTRY VISITED: Apart from my homeland, America.
FAVOURITE ACTOR/ACTRESS: Clint Eastwood/Lee Remick.
BEST FILM SEEN IN THE PAST YEAR: Indiana Jones and the Temple of Doom.

BEST FRIENDS: Too many to mention.
BIGGEST INFLUENCE ON CAREER: My family.
WHAT YOU DON'T LIKE ABOUT FOOTBALL: Losing.
SUPERSTITIONS: None.
PRE-MATCH MEAL: Steak.

INTERNATIONAL HONOURS: Nineteen full Eire caps.
PERSONAL AMBITION: To be happy and successful.
PROFESSIONAL AMBITION: To win the League with United and qualify for the World Cup Finals with Eire.
CAREER AFTER PLAYING: I'll probably go back to accountancy.
PLAYER FOR THE FUTURE: Martin Russell — a left-sided midfield player at Old Trafford.
ADVICE TO YOUNGSTERS: Work hard and enjoy your training.

1985-86

*UEFA's English ban, Liverpool's double
and The Hand Of God.*

1985-86

HAMMERS HITMAN!

October 19, 1985

Tommy Docherty believes Ron Atkinson's Man. United side is better than Sir Matt Busby's 1968 team as they shoot to the top of the table. The stars praise new West Ham striker Frank McAvennie, who scores ten in his first 11 league games.

U BEAUTIES!

April 26, 1986

Oxford cruise to Milk Cup glory with a 3-0 win over Jim Smith's 'diabolical' QPR side. John Aldridge sets up two of the goals, one for man of the match Trevor Hebberd who returns to Wembley after missing the 1979 League Cup final.

MERSEY MAGIC!

May 10, 1986

Liverpool's Jan Molby hits back at critics who say he's overweight by guiding The Reds to the first all-Merseyside FA Cup final. Everton keeper Bobby Mimms is set to play in goal with regular No.1 Neville Southall injured.

HAT-TRICK HERO!

June 21, 1986

There's great colour action from the World Cup as Gary Lineker's treble batters Poland in Monterrey. "To score any hat-trick is nice, but to do it in the Finals and join Geoff Hurst in the record books makes it special," he tells MATCH.

WORLD CHAMPS!

July 5, 1986

Argentina captain Diego Maradona kisses the World Cup in the sun-baked Azteca, while inside the future of England's strikeforce is debated following the success in Mexico of the Lineker-Beardsley partnership.

Gary Lineker

>> STAR PLAYERS!

GARY LINEKER, Everton: The Toffees' predatory striker had an amazing season – his only one with the Goodison club before moving to Barcelona. He made a big-money move to Merseyside from Leicester, scored 38 goals, reached an FA Cup final and then finished top scorer at the World Cup, helping England to the quarter-finals.

TONY COTTEE, West Ham: The tiny Hammers frontman formed a lethal forward pairing with Scotland international Frank McAvennie in 1985-86. The partnership produced 53 goals as John Lyall's side pushed Liverpool all the way in the league, but eventually finished third.

Tony Cottee

BEST KIT!
Everton's NEC home kit.

WORST KIT!
Newcastle's silver away kit.

≫ SEASON HIGHLIGHTS!

AUGUST: UEFA ban English teams from Europe indefinitely in the aftermath of the Heysel Stadium tragedy.

SEPTEMBER: Cash-strapped Charlton leave The Valley – their home for 66 years – and move in with Crystal Palace.

OCTOBER: Man United's ten game winning-streak ends as Luton hold the league leaders to a 1-1 draw.

NOVEMBER: Early-season strugglers West Ham climb to third in the table after beating West Brom 4-0.

DECEMBER: The Irish FA is refused permission by Nottingham Forest to interview Brian Clough for the vacant manager's position.

JANUARY: Swansea are given a 28-day winding-up order by the High Court and could be declared bankrupt at any time.

FEBRUARY: Everton regain top spot in Division One after Gary Lineker fires a hat-trick in a 4-0 win over Man. City.

MARCH: Don Howe quits as Arsenal boss following rumours of Terry Venables' interest in the Highbury job.

APRIL: Graeme Souness becomes player-manager at Ibrox after Rangers agree a £300,000 fee with Sampdoria.

MAY: Liverpool complete a League and FA Cup double, but have no English players in their Cup Final line-up.

JUNE: Diego Maradona leads Argentina to World Cup glory, beating West Germany 3-2.

KENNY PINCHER!

DALGLISH DECIDES TITLE RACE ...

SOCCER MOURNS THE 'BIG MAN'

GLORY FOR GARY

Clockwise from top: Liverpool player-manager Kenny Dalglish bags the title on the last day of the season, Gary Lineker wins the PFA Player Of The Year award, Oxford celebrate winning the Milk Cup and football mourns the death of Celtic legend Jock Stein.

MILK CUP FINAL '86

OXFORD DON THE CROWN!

≫ RISING STARS!

JOHN ALDRIDGE OXFORD

JOHN ALDRIDGE: The U's striker was instrumental in Oxford's first season in Division One. He was the third top scorer and hit six goals as Maurice Evans' side reached the last ever Milk Cup final.

PAUL GASCOIGNE: Under manager Willie McFaul, Gazza got his first start in a Newcastle shirt on the opening day of the season. He finished the campaign with nine league goals.

Above: The men who made history! The victorious Reds revel in the glory at the end of an amazing season.

● Pictures: Phil Bagnall and Lawrence Lustig.

FA CUP FINAL SPECIAL

Dalglish's Double diamonds!

SATURDAY'S FA Cup Final didn't just live up to pre-match expectations. It exceeded them!

The first all-Merseyside Final produced a match with just about everything — fierce tackles, flowing football, breathtaking saves and great goals.

History was made as Liverpool became only the third club this century to capture the League and Cup Double and Kenny Dalglish the first player-manager to win the FA Cup.

Everton hardly deserve to get nothing from a game in which they played such an inspiring part but, although it was Alan Hansen who climbed the Wembley steps to collect the trophy, football emerged as the real winner.

Below: Liverpool's Jim Beglin (left) and skipper Alan Hansen parade the FA Cup around Wembley after one of the finest Finals of recent years.

Above: Wembley belongs to Kenny Dalglish as the jubilant Liverpool boss — the first player-manager ever to win the FA Cup — hoists the trophy aloft to acclaim a remarkable League and Cup Double.

Bobby Robson — picked a young squad.

PETER SHILTON

Southampton. Born — Leicester, September 18, 1949; Caps — 79; Goals — nil; WORLD CUP PLUS — experienced and always reliable. One of the world's best 'keepers; MEXICO MINUS — none.

CHRIS WOODS

Norwich. Born — Boston, November 14, 1959; Caps — 3; Goals — nil; WORLD CUP PLUS — will have learned much from working under Peter Shilton; MEXICO MINUS — lacks experience of big occasion.

GARY BAILEY

Manchester United. Born — Ipswich, August 9, 1958; Caps — 2; Goals — nil; WORLD CUP PLUS — has played at the top level with one of the country's biggest clubs; MEXICO MINUS — threatened by injury and prone to inconsistency.

TERRY BUTCHER

Ipswich. Born — Singapore, December 28, 1958; Caps — 38; Goals — 3; WORLD CUP PLUS — dominant and assuring at the back, dangerous at set pieces; MEXICO MINUS — distribution could perhaps be improved.

ALVIN MARTIN

West Ham. Born — Liverpool, July 29, 1958; Caps — 14; Goals — nil; WORLD CUP PLUS — strong in the air and in the tackle. Ideal replacement for Terry Butcher; MEXICO MINUS — like Terry, his passing sometimes lets him down.

TERRY FENWICK

Queen's Park Rangers. Born — Sunderland, November 17, 1959; Caps — 14; Goals — nil; WORLD CUP PLUS — aggressive and strong in the tackle, a perfect defensive foil for Terry Butcher; MEXICO MINUS — prone to over-enthusiasm.

REPORTER *Dave Smith runs the rule over England's final 22 for the World Cup Finals.*

THE MEN

BOBBY Robson has turned to the 'Young Ones' to fulfil his Mexico dream.

But it's the likes of Trev, Steve and Mark rather than television's Viv, Neil and Mike on whom the England boss is pinning his hopes this summer. With the strength-sapping heat of Mexico in mind, he's bravely selected a youthful squad whose average age stands at just 26.

That's four years younger than the party former manager Ron Greenwood took to Spain in 1982!

Apart from 'keeper Peter Shilton, all Robson's men are under 30 with several of them in their early 20's and yet to reach their prime.

At the tender age of 22, John Barnes and Trevor Steven are the youngest members of a squad which also contains two 23-year-olds in Gary Stevens of Everton and newcomer Steve Hodge.

And with the England chief preferring a somewhat 'rookie' strike force — with only 75 caps between them — there's no place for the experienced Trevor Francis and Tony Woodcock.

Instead Newcastle sensation Peter Beardsley is given the nod as the Italian-based Francis is left to ponder over what might be the end of his England career.

While we sympathise with the Sampdoria striker, Peter says: "Obviously I'm very delighted —

GLENN HODDLE

Tottenham. Born — Hayes, October 27, 1957; Caps — 31; Goals — 8; WORLD CUP PLUS — his style should be ideally suited to the conditions in South America; MEXICO MINUS — can tend to drift out of game.

STEVE HODGE

Aston Villa. Born — Nottingham, October 25, 1962; Caps — 2; Goals — nil; WORLD CUP PLUS — proved against Scotland he's an excellent stand-in for Bryan Robson; MEXICO MINUS — still a novice at international level.

TREVOR STEVEN

Everton. Born — Berwick-upon-Tweed, September 21, 1963; Caps — 9; Goals — three; WORLD CUP PLUS — gives the side extra width and scope; MEXICO MINUS — sometimes neglects defensive responsibilities.

GARY LINEKER

Everton. Born — Leicester, November 30, 1960; Caps — 12; Goals — 6; WORLD CUP PLUS — his speed and clinical eye for goal will make him a handful for any defence; MEXICO MINUS — none.

MARK HATELEY

AC Milan. Born — Derby, November 7, 1961; Caps — 16; Goals — 6; WORLD CUP PLUS — powerful in the air. His reputation could frighten defenders; MEXICO MINUS — had a bad season with injuries and may not be 100 per cent fit.

PETER BEARDSLEY

Newcastle. Born — Newcastle, January 18, 1961; Caps — 3; Goals — nil; WORLD CUP PLUS — extremely skilful and currently possesses supreme confidence; MEXICO MINUS — only his lack of experience stands in his way.

GARY STEVENS

Everton. Born — Barrow, March 27, 1963; Caps — 8; Goals — nil; WORLD CUP PLUS — quick and dependable, good on the overlap; MEXICO MINUS — keenness to push forward sometimes leaves him exposed.

GARY STEVENS

Tottenham. Born — Hillingdon, March 30, 1962; Caps — 4; Goals — nil; WORLD CUP PLUS — his versatility makes him a valuable asset on the subs' bench; MEXICO MINUS — short on international experience.

VIV ANDERSON

Arsenal. Born — Nottingham, July 29, 1956. Caps — 20; Goals — 1; WORLD CUP PLUS — natural cover for Gary Stevens, good going forward; MEXICO MINUS — marking sometimes leaves a lot to be desired.

BRYAN ROBSON

Manchester United. Born — Chester-le-Street, January 11, 1957; Caps — 50; Goals — 18; WORLD CUP PLUS — an inspirational leader and always likely to score! MEXICO MINUS — shoulder and hamstring trouble could restrict him.

KENNY SANSOM

Arsenal. Born — London, September 26, 1958. Caps — 63; Goals — 1; WORLD CUP PLUS — probably England's most consistent outfield player; MEXICO MINUS — perhaps a little vulnerable on his right-hand side.

RAY WILKINS

AC Milan. Born — Hillingdon, September 14, 1956; Caps — 78; Goals — 3; WORLD CUP PLUS — experienced campaigner who possesses a valuable calming influence; MEXICO MINUS — sometimes too negative and doesn't score enough goals.

but it's a bit awkward knowing that I'm replacing Trevor Francis.

"I feel sorry for him. He's clearly a talented player who's done a lot for England in the past.

"As far as I'm concerned I'd always been hopeful of making the squad, but at no stage felt I was certain to be included.

"I've been lucky to come good at the right time and be picked to play in the last four England games before the Finals in Mexico."

As for sad Sampdoria star Trevor, it's a tragic end to a disastrous season littered with injury set-backs.

A fractured cheekbone looked set to keep him out of England's final warm-up game against Scotland, but he bravely chose to play in a last-ditch attempt to make the squad for Mexico.

Despite an all-action performance, his efforts were in vain and he was left to ask of his England manager: "What did I have to do to get in?"

Adds Trevor: "I can't understand why he brought me back into the team to play Scotland with a fractured cheekbone if I had no real chance of going to Mexico.

"I believe he has made a mistake in not going for more experience up front. I felt that

FOR MEXICO

ROBSON GOES FOR THE YOUNG ONES

PETER REID

Everton. Born — Huyton, June 20, 1956; Caps — 5; Goals — nil; WORLD CUP PLUS — a ball-winner who would complement Glenn Hoddle perfectly; MEXICO MINUS — injury problems this season could make him a risk.

KERRY DIXON

Chelsea. Born — Luton, July 24, 1961; Caps — 5; Goals — 4; WORLD CUP PLUS — good aerial target and always likely to score given the service; MEXICO MINUS — may lack confidence after a disappointing 1986 so far.

JOHN BARNES

Watford. Born — Jamaica, November 7, 1963; Caps — 25; Goals — 3; WORLD CUP PLUS — has the ability to turn a game with one flash of brilliance; MEXICO MINUS — unpredictable and inconsistent.

CHRIS WADDLE

Tottenham. Born — Gateshead, December 14, 1960; Caps — 14; Goals — 2; WORLD CUP PLUS — like his rival John Barnes has the talent to tear defences apart; MEXICO MINUS — may be lacking in self-belief.

either Tony Woodcock or I were sure to make the final squad.

"What real international experience have strikers like Mark Hateley, Gary Lineker, Kerry Dixon and Peter Beardsley got?"

Another disappointed player who will not be making the trip to Mexico is Norwich skipper Dave Watson.

Like Trevor he too played in the Stanley Rous Cup clash with Scotland and has also been placed on fitness alert this summer.

Little or no consolation there for the Liverpool-born centre-half who confesses: "I gave it all I had against the Scots, so to have come so close is upsetting.

"But I'm still relatively young and I've got to look to the future and that means the European Championship in two years' time and the next World Cup."

Yet by the 1990 Finals, the average age of the England squad will be the same as that which went to Spain four years ago. So it seems the men for Mexico could be around for a long time after.

● AS a safeguard against injury to any of his squad of 22, Bobby Robson has named six players who will be on stand-by.
They are: Mick Harford (Luton), Trevor Francis (Sampdoria), Dave Watson (Norwich), Stewart Robson (Arsenal), Martin Hodge (Sheffield Wednesday) and Paul Bracewell (Everton).

The goal of the tournament! Grounded Peter Shilton and England defenders Gary Stevens (left) and Terry Butcher (tackling) are powerless as Maradona puts Argentina 2-0 ahead.

England discover

DIEGO'S A HANDFUL!

DIEGO MARADONA raises his arms in triumph as the Argentine fans salute his two-goal blast against England. His controversial handled goal will be talked about for years, as will his superb solo effort (above left) which was hailed as the goal of the tournament.

Right: Caught red-handed! Diego Maradona clearly fists the ball over Peter Shilton for Argentina's first goal.

WORLD CUP SPECIAL

Gary Lineker gives England hope as he beats team-mate Terry Fenwick to the ball to head home a John Barnes cross and make the score 2-1.

ONE! Defender Jose Brown (right) leaps to open the scoring for Argentina with German 'keeper Harald Schumacher stranded.

THE WORLD CUP FINAL

ARGENTINA'S controversial World Cup campaign finally saw them showered in glory as they won over the hearts of the Mexican fans to lift the prized trophy for the second time in only eight years.

And in so doing, they thwarted West Germany's brave bid to become the first European team to win the trophy on South American soil.

It was Argentina, of course, who were labelled 'cheats' following skipper Diego Maradona's 'goal that never was' in the 2-1 Quarter-Final victory over England.

■ *NEXT WEEK: Special report on the world's number one Diego Maradona ... and the very best in colour action from the Azteca Stadium.*

WORLD CUP FINAL FACTS

	Argentina	W. Germany
SHOTS ON TARGET	6	3
SHOTS OFF TARGET	3	2
HEADERS ON TARGET	1	1
HEADERS OFF TARGET	1	1
CORNERS FOR	8	6
FREE-KICKS AGAINST	29	24
OFF-SIDES AGAINST	6	4

Vol. 7 No. 44

MATCH

Editorial
Stirling House, Bretton,
Peterborough PE3 8DJ
0733 260333

Editor: Melvyn Bagnall
News Editor: Paul Stratton
Reporters: Dave Smith, Louise Taylor
Photographer: Philip Bagnall
Production Editor: Mick Weavers
Design: Eric Jackson
Editor's secretary: Jacquie Apthorpe

Advertising
Bretton Court, Bretton,
Peterborough PE3 8DZ
0733 264666

Advert Executive: Brian Reacher
Advert secretary: Jackie Croote

Circulation
Bushfield House, Orton,
Peterborough PE2 0UW
0733 237111

Typeset by Typefont Ltd
Colour origination by
Lumarcolour

**Printed by the Riverside
Press, Whiddon Valley,
Barnstaple, Devon**

**Registered at the Post Office
as a newspaper**

© 1986 Pursuit Publishing (EMAP)

DIEGO'S

But there was nothing lucky about their subsequent Semi-Final victory over Belgium and tha acclamation of the earlier chastised Maradona as the world's number one player.

And in the Final itself, Argentina proved they were no one-man team when even the great Diego was forced to take an uncharacteristic back seat.

Carlos Bilardo's men seemed to have the trophy won as early as the 56th minute when the ever-dangerous Jorge Valdano gave them a 2-0 lead — adding to the earlier strike of defensive hero Jose Brown.

But the game exploded in the final fifteen minutes as first veteran Karl-Heinz Rummenigge and then Rudi Voeller struck from close range to level the score.

It was heart-stopping stuff but, almost inevitably, it was the South Americans who had the final say when Jorge Burruchaga scored the 132nd and final goal of the tournament to earn Argentina a 3-2 victory and turn the massed terraces of the giant Azteca Stadium into a sea of blue and white.

So Franz Beckenbauer's West German troops had to be content with runners-up spot for the second time in succession while Argentina returned to a heroes' welcome in Buenos Aires.

But Beckenbauer was gracious in defeat saying: "Argentina are a great team and they deserved to win.

"They had three good strikes on goal and scored three goals. We gambled in defence and, in the end, we were punished for

our mistakes."

Veteran players Karl-Heinz Rummenigge and Hans-Peter Briegel, however, criticised Germany's failure to sit back for the final few minutes after drawing level.

Said Rummenigge: "It was a big mistake to go on the attack after we had made the score 2-2. While it's a success to be losing Finalists, I'm very disappointed."

Added Briegel: "A side that plays as offensively as we did after drawing level does not deserve to win."

Argentina's defender Oscar Ruggeri admitted: "We got a bit worried after Germany levelled the scores and it was harder than we thought it would be. Thank goodness Burruchaga got that third goal!"

TWO! Jorge Valdano (centre) slips the ball past Schumacher to make the score 2-0.

Argentina skipper Diego Maradona holds the World Cup aloft following the dramatic victory over West Germany.

THREE! The World Cup winner coming up from Jorge Burruchaga (7) as he evades the challenge of defender Hans-Peter Briegel to make the score 3-2 to Argentina.

DAZZLERS

Karl-Heinz Rummenigge (11) pulls a goal back for Germany with a close-range effort in the 73rd minute.

No.1 PREBEN ELKJAER

WORLD SHAKERS

MEXICO 1986 has guaranteed Preben Elkjaer a place in football's hall of fame.

The classy 28-year-old Dane earned the right to be ranked alongside the greats of world soccer with a stunning hat-trick during his country's 6-1 hammering of fancied Uruguay and a string of pulsating performances.

And while Denmark crashed out of the tournament in a Second Round 5-1 disaster against Spain, their premature World Cup exit failed to stop Preben's up-front partnership with Michael Laudrup being dubbed: 'The best in the world'.

Preben has developed his scintillating speed and lethal reflexes in a hard school. At only 18, he was exported to Cologne and the tough, disciplined world of the German Bundesliga.

From there the Copenhagen-born goal king continued his nomadic existence with a spell in the rough and tumble of Belgian football at Lokeren before opting for Italy.

After only one season, Preben helped Verona clinch their first ever League Championship . . . and his country will be expecting further goal exploits in the European Championship, now less than two years away.

THE first in a super new colour series in which we spotlight the stars who shook the world in Mexico.

1986-87

*Houchen's header, Clive Allen's goals
and Man. United's Alex Ferguson.*

1986-87

Clive Allen

STAR PLAYERS!

CLIVE ALLEN, Tottenham: Until now the Spurs striker had failed to fulfil his early potential. Now playing up front on his own, with Glenn Hoddle, Chris Waddle and Ossie Ardiles supporting, Allen bagged 49 goals. He was sold a year later and never hit those heights again.

TONY ADAMS, Arsenal: The centre-back started the season on the fringes of the first-team. He finished it with an England cap and a League Cup winners' medal.

CLIVE ALLEN SPURS

Tony Adams

TITLE CHASERS!

August 23, 1986
MATCH predicts it will be Everton's season in the league, with Aston Villa in second and Liverpool third. Celebs have other ideas – The Pink Windmill's Grotbags reckons West Ham will win the lot, and Bobby Davro backs Spurs.

DEADLY DON!

December 27, 1986
Wimbledon's new signing Vinnie Jones talks to MATCH, just days after his winner against Man. United on his debut. The 21-year-old former hod carrier, who joined from Sweden's IFK Holmsund, says heading is his biggest strength.

REPLACING RUSH!

February 7, 1987
Liverpool finally sign 28-year-old John Aldridge, 14 years after they said they'd 'be in touch' after a trial. Down in the Vauxhall Conference, Scarborough boss Neil Warnock believes the best is yet to come from his promotion chasers.

HITSPURS!

April 11, 1987
After four years at Arsenal, Charlie Nicholas finally picks up a winners' medal in the Littlewoods Cup final. In MATCH Chat, Dave Smith reports that Glenn Hoddle and Chris Waddle are set to release a single called Diamond Lights.

FINAL FLING!

May 16, 1987
Glenn Hoddle hopes to end his Tottenham career by winning the FA Cup final, but Coventry striker Dave Bennett has other ideas. The former Man. City man wants a winners' medal to add to the losers' one he got in 1981, against Spurs.

BEST KIT!
Barcelona's classic home kit.

WORST KIT!
Tottenham's blue away kit.

>> SEASON HIGHLIGHTS!

JULY: Barcelona sign Everton's Gary Lineker for £2.2 million.

AUGUST: Northern Ireland's Colin Clarke nets a hat-trick on his Southampton debut.

SEPTEMBER: Division One newcomers Wimbledon go top after a 1-0 win over Watford.

OCTOBER: The FA support Luton's decision to ban away fans on the understanding that all other 91 league teams can ban Luton fans too.

NOVEMBER: Alex Ferguson is a popular choice as the ex-Aberdeen boss replaces Ron Atkinson at Old Trafford.

DECEMBER: Spurs defender Graham Roberts becomes Rangers' fifth English signing in six months, arriving at Ibrox in a £450,000 deal.

JANUARY: Man. United end Arsenal's 17-game unbeaten run in the league, sinking them 2-0 at Old Trafford.

FEBRUARY: Gary Lineker nets all England's goals in their 4-2 win over Spain.

MARCH: Ireland legend Liam Brady returns to England with West Ham in a £100,000 deal after seven seasons in Italy.

APRIL: Arsenal beat Liverpool 2-1 in the League Cup final – it's the first time in eight years that Ian Rush scores and Liverpool lose.

MAY: Coventry win an unforgettable FA Cup final, beating Spurs after extra-time.

JUNE: Ian Rush joins Juventus in a record £3.2 million deal.

Clockwise from top: The play-offs arrive in English football, Fulham are crushed 10-0 by Liverpool at Anfield in October, Everton seal the title by nine points and Barcelona new boy Gary Lineker hits two goals on his debut after moving from Goodison Park.

>> RISING STARS!

MATT LE TISSIER: The Guernsey-born playmaker broke into the Southampton first-team when he made his debut against Tottenham as a 17-year-old. Le Tiss didn't hit the net in his first match, but finished the season with six goals for The Saints.

DAVID ROCASTLE: Arsenal's No.7 missed just six league games and was in the Littlewoods Cup side that beat Liverpool just before his 20th birthday. 'Rocky' was PFA Young Player Of The Year runner-up.

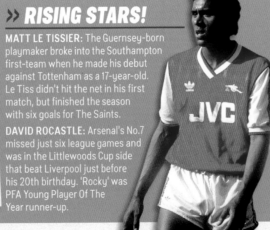

>> FINAL LEAGUE TABLES!

DIVISION ONE

	CLUB	P	W	D	L	F	A	GD	Pts
1.	Everton	42	26	8	8	76	31	+45	86
2.	Liverpool	42	23	8	11	72	42	+30	77
3.	Tottenham	42	21	8	13	68	43	+25	71
4.	Arsenal	42	20	10	12	58	35	+23	70
5.	Norwich	42	17	17	8	53	51	+2	68
6.	Wimbledon	42	19	9	14	57	50	+7	66
7.	Luton	42	18	12	12	47	45	+2	66
8.	Nott'm Forest	42	18	11	13	64	51	+13	65
9.	Watford	42	18	9	15	67	54	+13	63
10.	Coventry	42	17	12	13	50	45	+5	63
11.	Man. United	42	14	14	14	52	45	+7	56
12.	Southampton	42	14	10	18	69	68	+1	52
13.	Sheff. Wed.	42	13	13	16	58	59	-1	52
14.	Chelsea	42	13	13	16	53	64	-11	52
15.	West Ham	42	14	10	18	52	67	-15	52
16.	QPR	42	13	11	18	48	64	-16	50
17.	Newcastle	42	12	11	19	47	65	-18	47
18.	Oxford	42	11	13	18	44	69	-25	46
19.	Charlton	42	11	11	20	45	55	-10	44
20.	Leicester	42	11	9	22	54	76	-22	42
21.	Man. City	42	8	15	19	36	57	-21	39
22.	Aston Villa	42	8	12	22	45	79	-34	36

TOP SCORER: Clive Allen Tottenham, 33 goals

DIVISION TWO

	CLUB	P	W	D	L	F	A	GD	Pts
1.	Derby	42	25	9	8	64	38	+26	84
2.	Portsmouth	42	23	9	10	53	28	+25	78
3.	Oldham	42	22	9	11	65	44	+21	75
4.	Leeds	42	19	11	12	58	44	+14	68
5.	Ipswich	42	17	13	12	59	43	+16	64
6.	Crystal Palace	42	19	5	18	51	53	-2	62
7.	Plymouth	42	16	13	13	62	57	+5	61
8.	Stoke	42	16	10	16	63	53	+10	58
9.	Sheff. United	42	15	13	14	50	49	+1	58
10.	Bradford	42	15	10	17	62	62	0	55
11.	Barnsley	42	14	13	15	49	52	-3	55
12.	Blackburn	42	15	10	17	45	55	-10	55
13.	Reading	42	14	11	17	52	59	-7	53
14.	Hull	42	13	14	15	41	55	-14	53
15.	West Brom	42	13	12	17	51	49	+2	51
16.	Millwall	42	14	9	19	39	45	-6	51
17.	Huddersfield	42	13	12	17	54	61	-7	51
18.	Shrewsbury	42	15	6	21	41	53	-12	51
19.	Birmingham	42	11	17	14	47	59	-12	50
20.	Sunderland	42	12	12	18	49	59	-10	48
21.	Grimsby	42	10	14	18	39	59	-20	44
22.	Brighton	42	9	12	21	37	54	-17	39

TOP SCORER: Micky Quinn Portsmouth, 22 goals

DIVISION THREE

	CLUB	P	W	D	L	F	A	GD	Pts
1.	Bournemouth	46	29	10	7	76	40	+36	97
2.	Middlesbrough	46	28	10	8	67	30	+37	94
3.	Swindon	46	25	12	9	77	47	+30	87
4.	Wigan	46	25	10	11	83	60	+23	85
5.	Gillingham	46	23	9	14	65	48	+17	78
6.	Bristol City	46	21	14	11	63	36	+27	77
7.	Notts County	46	21	13	12	77	56	+21	76
8.	Walsall	46	22	9	15	80	67	+13	75
9.	Blackpool	46	16	16	14	74	59	+15	64
10.	Mansfield	46	15	16	15	52	55	-3	61
11.	Brentford	46	15	15	16	64	66	-2	60
12.	Port Vale	46	15	12	19	76	70	+6	57
13.	Doncaster	46	14	15	17	56	62	-6	57
14.	Rotherham	46	15	12	19	48	57	-9	57
15.	Chester	46	13	17	16	61	59	+2	56
16.	Bury	46	14	13	19	54	60	-6	55
17.	Chesterfield	46	13	15	18	56	69	-13	54
18.	Fulham	46	12	17	17	59	77	-18	53
19.	Bristol Rovers	46	13	12	21	49	75	-26	51
20.	York	46	12	13	21	55	79	-24	49
21.	Bolton	46	10	15	21	46	58	-12	45
22.	Carlisle	46	10	8	28	39	78	-39	38
23.	Darlington	46	7	16	23	45	77	-32	37
24.	Newport	46	8	13	25	49	86	-37	37

TOP SCORER: Andy Jones Port Vale, 29 goals

DIVISION FOUR

	CLUB	P	W	D	L	F	A	GD	Pts
1.	Northampton	46	30	9	7	103	53	+50	99
2.	Preston	46	26	12	8	72	47	+25	90
3.	Southend	46	25	5	16	68	55	+13	80
4.	Wolves	46	24	7	15	69	50	+19	79
5.	Colchester	46	21	7	18	64	56	+8	70
6.	Aldershot	46	20	10	16	64	57	+7	70
7.	Orient	46	20	9	17	64	61	+3	69
8.	Scunthorpe	46	18	12	16	73	57	+16	66
9.	Wrexham	46	15	20	11	70	51	+19	65
10.	Peterborough	46	17	14	15	57	50	+7	65
11.	Cambridge	46	17	11	18	60	62	-2	62
12.	Swansea	46	17	11	18	56	61	-5	62
13.	Cardiff	46	15	16	15	48	50	-2	61
14.	Exeter	46	11	23	12	53	49	+4	56
15.	Halifax	46	15	10	21	59	74	-15	55
16.	Hereford	46	14	11	21	60	61	-1	53
17.	Crewe	46	13	14	19	70	72	-2	53
18.	Hartlepool	46	11	18	17	44	65	-21	51
19.	Stockport	46	13	12	21	40	69	-29	51
20.	Tranmere	46	11	17	18	54	72	-18	50
21.	Rochdale	46	11	17	18	54	73	-19	50
22.	Burnley	46	12	13	21	53	74	-21	49
23.	Torquay	46	10	18	18	56	72	-16	48
24.	Lincoln	46	12	12	22	45	65	-20	48

TOP SCORER: Richard Hill Northampton, 28 goals

SCOTTISH correspondent Robert Watt talks to Rangers 'keeper Chris Woods about his bitter-sweet record-breaking achievement – and the man who spoiled his celebration party … EXCLUSIVE!

Chris Woods – "The record doesn't mean anything now."

Adrian Sprott – the Hamilton hero who ended Rangers' dream of the treble.

SHOT OUT!

HAMILTON hero Adrian Sprott forced quite a number of people to re-think their plans after his goal dramatically dumped Rangers out of the Scottish Cup.

When the 24-year-old clerical worker cashed in on a mistake by 'Light Blues' defender Dave McPherson, he:

● SUNK Rangers' hopes of winning the treble.

● HALTED Chris Woods' record-breaking run.

● SENT thousands of Rangers fans into mourning.

● RUINED his wife's plans of a quiet night at the cinema.

Instead of seeing Paul Hogan starring in the block-busting film 'Crocodile Dundee', Mrs Sprott was press-ganged into attending an impromptu champagne reception at Hamilton's Douglas Park ground.

It's safe to assume a grand time was had by all and Adrian says: "Who's to say we didn't deserve it?

"This has been a hard season for the club and there have been times when it looked as if fate was determined to mock us at every turn.

"But amidst it all, we had a feeling that our luck was about to change. Mind you, the prospect of winning at Ibrox was pretty remote. At best I fancied us to get a draw.

"However, the longer the game went on the more our confidence grew and when Dave McPherson took his eye off the ball and it broke to me in the penalty box I just let fly and hoped for the best."

It's history now that the ball crashed into the net to mark a memorable day in Adrian's life – and complete a personal revenge mission.

He explains: "A few years ago I was in the Meadowbank team which got to the Semi-Finals of the League Cup only to be beaten by Rangers.

"They won 5-1 on aggregate but, over the two games, the scoreline was a travesty of justice and flattered Rangers. Losing in such a manner was depressing and the rest of the season was an anti-climax.

"But winning at Ibrox with Hamilton has more than made up for that disappointment and I'm sure people will be talking about that win – and my goal – for a long time to come."

SHUT OUT!

BREAKING Bobby Clark's shut-out record should have been a proud achievement for Chris Woods.

Instead it mattered not a jot for the Rangers 'keeper who laments: "The game will be remembered as the day we were knocked out of the Cup and not as the day I set a new record.

"Believe me, I would be much happier if Hamilton had scored an early goal to end my record hopes and then we hit back to win 2-1.

"So all I want to do is forget about it and concentrate on helping Rangers pick ourselves up and climb to the top of the table."

Before Chris was beaten by Adrian Sprott's 70th-minute shot, he had kept his goal intact for a total of 1,196 minutes – a run stretching back to the 44th minute of the 'Light Blues' UEFA Cup tie with Borussia Moenchengladbach.

That was on November 26 and the England international went on to complete 12½ games without conceding a goal.

When he passed the 30-minute mark against Hamilton with the scoresheet still blank, he took over the record set by Aberdeen's Bobby Clark back in the 1970/71 season.

Prior to that game, Chris had also achieved another shut-out target. At the start of the season he told MATCH readers that he had his sights set on keeping 20 clean sheets in his first term with Rangers.

Seventeen blanks in the Premier League and three in the UEFA Cup gave him that score.

■ IT'S 21 years since Dundee United beat Barcelona in their first-ever European tie, and here's how they have fared since:-

Season	Competition	Progress
1966-67	Fairs Cup	Third Round
1969-70	Fairs Cup	First Round
1970-71	Fairs Cup	Second Round
1974-75	Cup Winners' Cup	Second Round
1975-76	UEFA Cup	Second Round
1977-78	UEFA Cup	First Round
1978-79	UEFA Cup	First Round
1979-80	UEFA Cup	Second Round
1980-81	UEFA Cup	Second Round
1981-82	UEFA Cup	Quarter-Finals
1982-83	UEFA Cup	Quarter-Finals
1983-84	European Cup	Semi-Finals
1984-85	UEFA Cup	Third Round
1985-86	UEFA Cup	Third Round

DUNDEE UNITED'S heart-warming victory over Terry Venables' multi-million pound Barcelona team in the awesome Nou Camp Stadium ranks alongside the best of British successes on foreign soil. And, as the 'Terrors of Tannadice' returned home after the sensation in Spain, Scottish correspondent Robert Watt was there to greet them … EXCLUSIVE!

GOAL-STOPPER John Clark turned goal-getter to crown the most memorable night of his life.

Having combined with defenders Paul Hegarty and David Narey to snuff out the threat of Barcelona's British strikers Gary Lineker and Mark Hughes, he popped up at the other end to clinch a place in the Semi-Finals against Borussia Moenchengladbach.

And as he basked in the glory of United's greatest-ever European victory, he recalled how he numbed the Nou Camp.

"Getting my head to Iain Redford's free-kick was the sweetest moment of my career," enthuses the 22-year-old central defender.

"And it is indicative of our control of the game that I was able to move out of defence to get our equaliser.

"A lot of credit must go to Iain Redford for the precision of his cross. All I had to do was move in front of my marker and get my header on target.

"Coming with only five minutes to go, it really finished the tie, but it was nice to see Iain Ferguson stick another one in for good measure."

It completed a miserable night for Barcelona boss Terry Venables who had seen his £5 million signings Gary Lineker and Mark Hughes reduced to spectators.

Apart from one golden opportunity in the first leg at Tannadice and a half-chance in the Nou Camp, the England international was kept very quiet by United's five-man defence.

Says John: "Gary and Mark have come in for a lot of criticism for their lack of success against us but, in fairness to them, we were right on top of our job and didn't give them a moment's freedom."

Yet while John turned out to be the hero of the hour, it wasn't until the day before the game that he was certain of actually playing.

"In the days leading up to the game, I was aware of speculation that, with Paul Hegarty fully fit again, I would have to settle for a seat on the bench," he says.

"But with Eamonn Bannon failing a late fitness test, the door opened once more and gave me the opportunity to enjoy a memorable night."

'WE WERE MAGNIFICENT' – McLEAN

DUNDEE UNITED manager Jim McLean couldn't hide his delight as he poured praise on his UEFA Cup heroes.

And while often reluctant to single out individuals for special mention, he was forced to concede: "Paul Sturrock was superb over both legs.

"He tore them apart and had a major influence on what is surely our greatest result in Europe. But every single player in our side was magnificent.

"In the past I have perhaps been too inclined to play down our achievements but no praise is high enough for the players who have taken the club to another European Semi-Final.

"And while I remain reluctant to come straight out and say we will now go on to win the UEFA Cup, we are certainly well placed to go all the way."

With only a single goal advantage from the first leg at Tannadice, Jim knew he couldn't let his side sit back and defend the slender lead.

He says: "We set out to take the game to Barcelona and get another goal and, although we lost one at a bad time, I was always confident of getting a result.

"And even with extra-time staring us in the face with five minutes to go, I was looking forward to it with the same confidence.

"We will never face a tougher test than we did in Barcelona – and I'm very proud that we came through with flying colours."

UNITED BLAST BARCELONA

DUNDEE DYNAMITE!

Goal heroes John Clark (right) and Iain Ferguson are joined by Kevin Gallacher as Dundee United celebrate a magical night in the Nou Camp Stadium.

SCARBOROUGH

MITCH'S MEN STORM INTO THE LEAGUE

MITCH COOK is thrilled to have seen his teenage dream come true.

The Scarborough-born-and-bred striker kicked off his soccer career with 'The Boro' as a 17-year-old, nurturing fantasies of one day playing League soccer at the Athletic Ground.

And the 25-year-old enthuses: "I first joined Scarborough just after they'd gone through the glory days of the 1970s and my ambition was always to play in the League for the club. This is a dream come true!"

Mitch quit Scarborough in 1984 to pursue a League career with first Darlington, whom he helped to promotion to Division Three in 1985, and then Middlesbrough.

However, after making only half-a-dozen first team appearances at Ayresome Park early in the 1985-86 season, Mitch returned to his native Scarborough and his former job as a bus driver, reclaiming his old place in 'The Boro' attack.

However, even Mitch didn't anticipate that his first season back at the Athletic Ground would prove so successful.

"When we learned that there would be automatic promotion, we immediately made reaching the Fourth Division our ambition but, that said, I didn't really expect it to happen in the first season. Going up this time has been a real bonus," says Mitch.

Along with Mitch, several Scarborough players already have valuable League experience under their belts. All were at one point discarded by their various League teams and all feel they have points to prove.

As Mitch puts it: "We're all delighted to be back and, along with a few others, I feel I've got a point to prove to certain people."

One of Scarborough's former League players is 25-year-old defender Steve Richards, who, along with spells at Hull, York and Cambridge, spent part of last season at Lincoln City.

All smiles from Mitch Cook as Miss Scarborough, Carolyn Hodgson (17), adds a touch of glamour to the occasion.

The Sincil Bank club are, of course, the unfortunate team to have finished 92nd in the League and thus replace Scarborough in the Vauxhall Conference.

And Mitch has a considerable depth of feeling towards Lincoln's plight, stressing: "We all have a lot of sympathy for Lincoln and Steve Richards feels particularly sad."

However, Mitch has no fears that Scarborough will go Lincoln's way in twelve months' time: "I've got no doubts about our ability to do well. I don't believe the Fourth Division is really much different from the Vauxhall Conference.

"Our only doubt has got to be how we will cope as part-timers, but I believe that some of the players will turn full-time and I wouldn't mind doing so," says the man who hit 15 Vauxhall Conference goals this term.

Whether or not 'The Boro' will succeed as a team of part-timers remains to be seen but, for the moment, they are solely concentrating on celebrating their success."

"The night after winning the Vauxhall Conference, we had a special dinner and a great night out followed by a champagne breakfast. Then there was a civic reception and an open-top bus tour round the town," enthuses Mitch.

With the Scarborough players currently soaking up the Spanish sunshine, the VIP treatment continues but, come August, the Fourth Division counterparts will be out to spoil the party.

SEASIDE SENSATIONS REALISE A DREAM

AMBITIOUS Scarborough, desperate for League status, once made an amazing takeover bid for struggling Halifax Town with the intention of moving them, lock, stock and barrel to their Athletic Ground home.

But Halifax just didn't want to be beside the seaside. The football authorities blocked the move and Scarborough were thwarted.

That was a few years ago but then, at the start of this season, the much-travelled Neil Warnock took over as the coastal club's boss and, retaining just two players, set about a massive rebuilding operation.

And ironically it was to The Shay that the former Burton Albion boss turned for inspiration and new faces. In came Ray McHale, Cec Podd, Paul Kendall, Tommy Graham, Stewart Mell and Barry Gallagher – all former Halifax players.

The latter's stay was a brief one before the midfield man settled for life in Malta but the rest, well supported by some talented youngsters, took the non-League scene by storm.

The manager's aim from the outset was not only to bring back the glory days of the 1970s, when Scarborough went to Wembley four times in five years and returned home with the FA Trophy three times, but to claim a place in the Fourth Division by right.

And with the introduction of automatic promotion from the Vauxhall Conference providing the juicy carrot dangling before their noses, 'The Boro' overcame a faltering start to put together a record-breaking 22-match unbeaten run to pip hot favourites Barnet at the post.

Skipper Cec Podd (34) – the man who with 502 League appearances set the Bradford City record before moving on to Halifax – is certain his new club can go on to better things.

"We've certainly got the footballing ability," he enthuses.

Manager Neil Warnock – rebuilt the side.

Cec Podd – looking ahead.

"The lads are also very fit but the big difference in the Fourth Division will be the fitness you get from the full-time training. And while our chairman has said he wants to pioneer part-time football in the League, I would expect some of our players to make the switch.

"Not all of them want it because they have good jobs and I can't exactly say what my situation will be at the moment but I'll definitely be at Scarborough and really looking forward to Fourth Division football again."

FLAIR!

DIVISION FOUR HERE WE COME! Little Scarborough became the first club to win automatic promotion to the Football League when they clinched the Vauxhall Conference title at the expense of long-time favourites Barnet. And here MATCH pays tribute to the proud Yorkshire set-up who will take the place of Lincoln in the big time next season . . .

Mitch Cook, complete with straw boater, celebrates with the GM Vauxhall Conference Championship trophy.

● **NEXT WEEK: WHERE TO NOW FOR LINCOLN? SPECIAL REPORT.**

Charlie Nicholas (10) sees his deflected shot win the Littlewoods Cup and (below) he sidefoots Arsenal's equaliser.

CHARLIE ENDS

Jubilant Arsenal pose for photographers after their Littlewoods Cup win.

THE RUSH LEGEND

NICHOLAS STRIKES TWICE FOR WEMBLEY GLORY

LITTLEWOODS CUP FINAL SPECIAL

CHEERFUL Charlie Nicholas brought smiles as wide as the marble halls of Highbury with a two-goal blast to win the first Littlewoods Cup. But while the Arsenal striker celebrated his match-winning performance, Italian-bound Ian Rush was mourning the end of an era as Liverpool were beaten for the first time in a game which he's scored. Now turn to Page 4.

Tony Adams (6) closes in on Ian Rush and John Lukic prepares to dive but they can't stop the Liverpool ace putting his side ahead mid-way through the first-half.

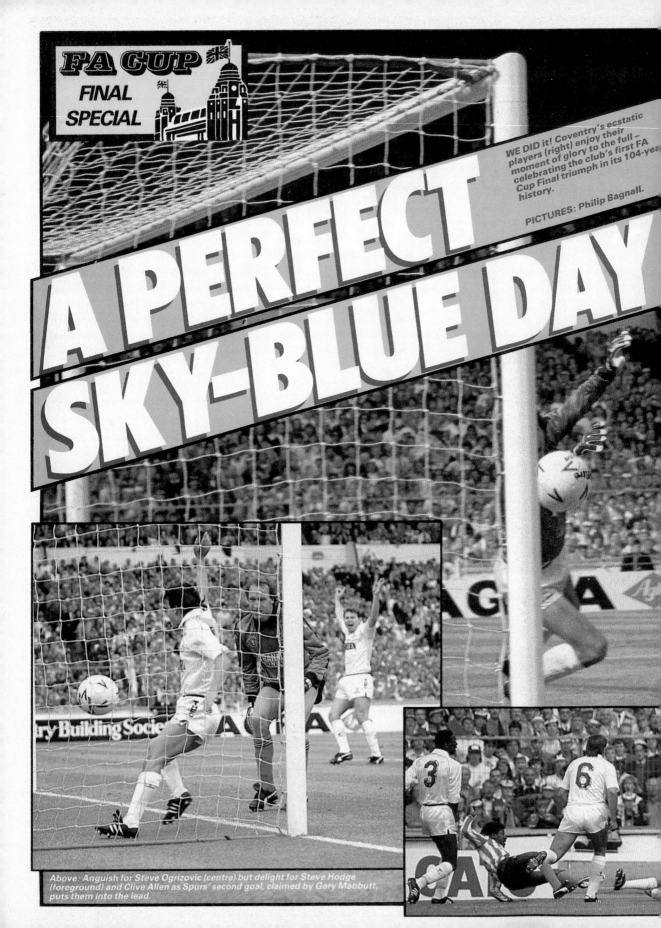

WE DID it! Coventry's ecstatic players (right) enjoy their moment of glory to the full – celebrating the club's first FA Cup Final triumph in its 104-year history.

PICTURES: Philip Bagnall.

A PERFECT SKY-BLUE DAY

Above: Anguish for Steve Ogrizovic (centre) but delight for Steve Hodge (foreground) and Clive Allen as Spurs' second goal, claimed by Gary Mabbutt, puts them into the lead.

classic goal for a classic Final! Keith Houchen is still flying through the air as his dynamic diving header crashes past Ray Clemence into the Spurs' net, making the score 2-2.

Coventry are level! Dave Bennett (second left) guides the ball past Ray Clemence for a sensational equaliser after Clive Allen had opened the scoring for Spurs.

FULL NAME: Niall John Quinn.
BIRTHPLACE/DATE: Dublin/October 6, 1966.
HEIGHT/WEIGHT: 6ft 4ins/13st 5lbs.
MARRIED: No.

THE PRIVATE LIFE OF..
ARSENAL'S
NIALL QUINN

WHAT IS YOUR FAVOURITE ARTICLE OF CLOTHING AND WHY? My jeans and a sweatshirt because they're so comfortable.

WHO ARE YOUR MOST FAMOUS FRIENDS OUTSIDE FOOTBALL? Professional darts players Bob Anderson and Terry O'Dea.

WHAT SUBJECT DID YOU HATE MOST AT SCHOOL? Science – the words were a bit too long and complicated for my liking.

WHAT WOULD YOU DO IF YOU COULD BE INVISIBLE FOR A DAY? Spend it inside John Lukic's wallet to see how much he really takes out with him.

WHAT WOULD YOU DO IF SOMEONE GAVE YOU £50,000 TODAY? Buy myself a brand new car … and I'm sure it wouldn't take me long to spend the rest.

WHAT IS YOUR CLAIM TO FAME OUTSIDE FOOTBALL? I represented Ireland at Gaelic football on a tour of Australia when I was 16. I almost took up the sport professionally before Arsenal came in for me.

HOW MANY 'O' LEVELS DID YOU GET? I got the Irish equivalent of eight in English, Irish language, Maths, History, Geography, Commerce, Science and French.

WHO WOULD YOU MOST LIKE TO MEET AND WHY? The Pope – because he holds such a special place in Irish homes.

WHAT, IF ANYTHING, FRIGHTENS YOU? Charlie Nicholas in the morning at training. He sneaks up behind you and screams in your ear to make sure you're awake – and I'm usually still half asleep.

WHAT WAS THE FIRST CAR YOU BOUGHT AND HOW MUCH DID IT COST? I haven't bought one yet because I haven't passed my driving test, but I'm working at it … slowly!

WHO ARE YOUR FAVOURITE POP STARS? They're hardly pop stars but I like Shirley Bassey and Frank Sinatra.

WHAT DO YOU WANT FOR YOUR BIRTHDAY? A new pair of training shoes because my old ones are getting a bit tatty.

WHAT IS YOUR FAVOURITE POSSESSION AT HOME? My bed and my alarm clock!

WHAT DON'T YOU LIKE ABOUT YOURSELF? My laziness. Since I started training every day, I get very tired.

OUTSIDE FOOTBALL, WHAT IS THE BIGGEST RISK YOU HAVE EVER TAKEN? Going mountain climbing with other Arsenal apprentices in Snowdonia, when I froze half way up (literally).

DO YOU HAVE ANY HOBBIES? Relaxing sports like golf and snooker and playing cards before a game.

WHICH DAY OF THE WEEK DO YOU DISLIKE MOST? Fridays, because you can't do anything apart from prepare for Saturday's game.

IF YOU COULD BE A FLY ON THE WALL, WHERE WOULD YOU MOST LIKE TO BE? Inside Charlie Nicholas's flat to see what sort of crazy antics he gets up to.

HAVE YOU EVER BEEN MISTAKEN FOR ANYONE ELSE? Yes, my Arsenal team-mate David O'Leary.

IF YOU WERE COMPETING IN MASTERMIND, WHAT WOULD YOUR SPECIALIST SUBJECT BE? Irish history.

WHO IS YOUR FAVOURITE CARTOON CHARACTER? Fred Flintstone.

WHAT IS YOUR IDEA OF RELAXATION? Watching a good film on my video – either the 'Pink Panther' movies or the old black and white classics.

IF YOU WERE FORCED TO SEEK A NEW JOB TOMORROW, WHAT WOULD YOU DO? Go back to Ireland and become a farmer.

WHICH OTHER SPORTSMEN WOULD YOU MOST LIKE TO BE AND WHY? Either a flamboyant Steve Davis or the golfer Greg Norman – I'm the right height and build, but the similarity ends there.

WHICH ACTOR WOULD YOU MOST LIKE TO BE AND WHY? Clint Eastwood, so that everyone would stand and stare when I walked in the room.

DO YOU HAVE ANY RECURRING DREAMS? Yes, ever since Villa knocked us out of last season's Milk Cup, I've dreamed that my shot which hit the bar actually went in and we went through instead of them.

1987-88

*The Crazy Gang, Newcastle's
Samba star and Euro '88.*

1987-88

BEARDO 'N' BARNES!

November 21, 1987

England qualify for the European Championship Finals after thrashing Yugoslavia 4-1 in Belgrade. Goalscoring ace Gary Lineker declares: "We can win it! We're strong enough and have proved we are a team to be feared."

STUNNING STEIN!

April 30, 1988

Luton's two-goal hero Brian Stein lifts the League Cup as The Hatters come from 2-1 down to beat Arsenal. Stand-in goalkeeper Andy Dibble reveals he was only asked to replace Les Sealey just hours before kick-off.

FA CUP SHOCK!

May 21, 1988

The Crazy Gang wreck Liverpool's double dream as part-time wine bar boss Lawrie Sanchez scores the only goal of the FA Cup final. Dons keeper Dave Beasant saves a penalty from John Aldridge then lifts the trophy as captain.

AWESOME IRELAND!

June 18, 1988

A Ray Houghton header gives Ireland their first win over England for 39 years. The Liverpool midfielder scores after six minutes and tells MATCH: "It's only the second headed goal of my career. The first was in the FA Cup last season."

DEADLY DUTCH!

July 2, 1988

AC Milan team-mates Ruud Gullit and Marco van Basten inspire Holland to Euro '88 victory. MATCH columnist Emlyn Hughes tells Bobby Robson to bring Des Walker, Nigel Clough and Paul Gascoigne into the England squad.

John Barnes

>> STAR PLAYERS!

JOHN BARNES, Liverpool: The England winger had a brilliant first season at Anfield after his £900,000 move from Watford. He bagged 15 goals from midfield as Liverpool raced to the Division One title and were narrowly beaten by Wimbledon in the FA Cup final.

PAUL GASCOIGNE, Newcastle: It took another two years before Gazza became a national icon, but he started making strides in an impressive campaign. Gascoigne was the new Chris Waddle, who tricked and teased opponents before joining Spurs that summer.

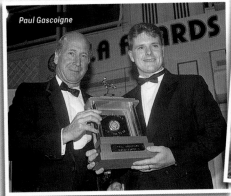

Paul Gascoigne

BEST KIT!

Liverpool's Crown Paints home kit.

WORST KIT!

Soviet Union home kit.

>> SEASON HIGHLIGHTS!

JULY: Liverpool splash out an English record £1.9 million for Newcastle's Peter Beardsley.

AUGUST: Barclays Bank agree a £5 million sponsorship deal with the Football League.

SEPTEMBER: Ten months after he was sacked by United, Ron Atkinson is named as West Brom's new manager.

OCTOBER: Terry Venables returns to England as manager of Spurs after being sacked by Spanish giants Barcelona.

NOVEMBER: England beat Yugoslavia 4-1 in a European Championship qualifier, netting all four goals in the first 24 minutes.

DECEMBER: Man. United pay an impressive £800,000 to bring Norwich centre-back Steve Bruce to Old Trafford.

JANUARY: Division One's bottom side Watford sack manager Dave Bassett after only six months.

FEBRUARY: UEFA uphold their decision to ban English clubs from European competitions for another season.

MARCH: Liverpool's 37-game unbeaten run ends at the hands of rivals Everton.

APRIL: Luton are the surprise winners of the League Cup, beating Arsenal 3-2.

MAY: Underdogs Wimbledon stop Liverpool winning the 'double, double' with a 1-0 win in the FA Cup final.

JUNE: Holland beat the USSR 2-0 in the Euro '88 final.

Clockwise from top: Brazilian Mirandinha arrives on Tyneside, Terry Venables returns to Division One, Ray Houghton's header gives Ireland a massive win in Stuttgart and Ian Rush plays his only season at Juventus before returning home.

>> RISING STARS!

IAN WRIGHT AND MARK BRIGHT: Crystal Palace's strikers took Division Two by storm, scoring 27 goals until Brighty's broken arm brought an end to their hot streak.

ALAN SHEARER: The Southampton striker broke Jimmy Greaves' 30-year-old record when, aged 17 years and 240 days, he became the youngest player to score a hat-trick in the top flight.

>> FINAL LEAGUE TABLES!

DIVISION ONE

	CLUB	P	W	D	L	F	A	GD	Pts
1	Liverpool	40	26	12	2	87	24	+63	90
2	Man. United	40	23	12	5	71	38	+33	81
3	Nott'm Forest	40	20	13	7	67	39	+28	73
4	Everton	40	19	13	8	53	27	+26	70
5	QPR	40	19	10	11	48	38	+10	67
6	Arsenal	40	18	12	10	58	39	+19	66
7	Wimbledon	40	14	15	11	58	47	+11	57
8	Newcastle	40	14	14	12	55	53	+2	56
9	Luton	40	14	11	15	57	58	-1	53
10	Coventry	40	13	14	13	46	53	-7	53
11	Sheff. Wed.	40	15	8	17	52	66	-14	53
12	Southampton	40	12	14	14	49	53	-4	50
13	Tottenham	40	12	11	17	38	48	-10	47
14	Norwich	40	12	9	19	40	52	-12	45
15	Derby	40	10	13	17	35	45	-10	43
16	West Ham	40	9	15	16	40	52	-12	42
17	Charlton	40	9	15	16	38	52	-14	42
18	Chelsea	40	9	15	16	50	68	-18	42
19	Portsmouth	40	7	14	19	36	66	-30	35
20	Watford	40	7	11	22	27	51	-24	32
21	Oxford	40	6	13	21	44	80	-36	31

TOP SCORER: John Aldridge *Liverpool, 26 goals*

DIVISION TWO

	CLUB	P	W	D	L	F	A	GD	Pts
1	Millwall	44	25	7	12	72	52	+20	82
2	Aston Villa	44	22	12	10	68	41	+27	78
3	Middlesbrough	44	22	12	10	63	36	+27	78
4	Bradford	44	22	11	11	74	54	+20	77
5	Blackburn	44	21	14	9	68	52	+16	77
6	Crystal Palace	44	22	9	13	86	59	+27	75
7	Leeds	44	19	12	13	61	51	+10	69
8	Ipswich	44	19	9	16	61	52	+9	66
9	Man. City	44	19	8	17	80	60	+20	65
10	Oldham	44	18	11	15	72	64	+8	65
11	Stoke	44	17	11	16	50	57	-7	62
12	Swindon	44	16	11	17	73	60	+13	59
13	Leicester	44	16	11	17	62	61	+1	59
14	Barnsley	44	15	12	17	61	62	-1	57
15	Hull	44	14	15	15	54	60	-6	57
16	Plymouth	44	16	8	20	65	67	-2	56
17	Bournemouth	44	13	10	21	56	68	-12	49
18	Shrewsbury	44	11	16	17	42	54	-12	49
19	Birmingham	44	11	15	18	41	66	-25	48
20	West Brom	44	12	11	21	50	69	-19	47
21	Sheff. United	44	13	7	24	45	74	-29	46
22	Reading	44	10	12	22	44	70	-26	42
23	Huddersfield	44	6	10	28	41	100	-59	28

TOP SCORER: David Currie *Barnsley, 28 goals*

DIVISION THREE

	CLUB	P	W	D	L	F	A	GD	Pts
1	Sunderland	46	27	12	7	92	48	+44	93
2	Brighton	46	23	15	8	69	47	+22	84
3	Walsall	46	23	13	10	68	50	+18	82
4	Notts County	46	23	12	11	82	49	+33	81
5	Bristol City	46	21	12	13	77	62	+15	75
6	Northampton	46	18	19	9	70	51	+19	73
7	Wigan	46	20	12	14	70	61	+9	72
8	Bristol Rovers	46	18	12	16	68	56	+12	66
9	Fulham	46	19	9	18	69	60	+9	66
10	Blackpool	46	17	14	15	71	62	+9	65
11	Port Vale	46	18	11	17	58	56	+2	65
12	Brentford	46	16	14	16	53	59	-6	62
13	Gillingham	46	14	17	15	77	61	+16	59
14	Bury	46	15	14	17	58	57	+1	59
15	Chester	46	14	16	16	51	62	-11	58
16	Preston	46	15	13	18	48	59	-11	58
17	Southend	46	14	13	19	65	83	-18	55
18	Chesterfield	46	15	10	21	41	70	-29	55
19	Mansfield	46	14	12	20	48	59	-11	54
20	Aldershot	46	15	8	23	64	74	-10	53
21	Rotherham	46	12	16	18	50	66	-16	52
22	Grimsby	46	12	14	20	48	58	-10	50
23	York	46	8	9	29	48	91	-43	33
24	Doncaster	46	8	9	29	40	84	-44	33

TOP SCORER: David Crown *Southend, 26 goals*

DIVISION FOUR

	CLUB	P	W	D	L	F	A	GD	Pts
1	Wolves	46	27	9	10	82	43	+39	90
2	Cardiff	46	24	13	9	66	41	+25	85
3	Bolton	46	22	12	12	66	42	+24	78
4	Scunthorpe	46	20	17	9	76	51	+25	77
5	Torquay	46	21	14	11	66	41	+25	77
6	Swansea	46	20	10	16	62	56	+6	70
7	Peterborough	46	20	10	16	52	53	-1	70
8	Leyton Orient	46	19	12	15	85	63	+22	69
9	Colchester	46	19	10	17	47	51	-4	67
10	Burnley	46	20	7	19	57	62	-5	67
11	Wrexham	46	20	6	20	69	58	+11	66
12	Scarborough	46	17	14	15	56	48	+8	65
13	Darlington	46	18	11	17	71	69	+2	65
14	Tranmere	46	19	9	18	61	53	+8	64
15	Cambridge	46	16	13	17	50	52	-2	61
16	Hartlepool	46	15	14	17	50	57	-7	59
17	Crewe	46	13	19	14	57	53	+4	58
18	Halifax	46	14	14	18	54	59	-5	55
19	Hereford	46	14	12	20	41	59	-18	54
20	Stockport	46	12	19	15	44	58	-14	51
21	Rochdale	46	11	15	20	47	76	-29	48
22	Exeter	46	11	13	22	53	68	-15	46
23	Carlisle	46	12	8	26	57	86	-29	44
24	Newport	46	6	7	33	35	105	-70	25

TOP SCORER: Steve Bull *Wolves, 34 goals*

LIVER[...]

SALUTE THE RED RECORD CHASERS

ON THE RUN

● Only four Liverpool players were ever-present during the 29-game unbeaten run ... Steve McMahon, John Barnes, Alan Hansen and Steve Nicol.

● Liverpool hammered four goals past their opponents on NINE occasions during the run ... achieving the feat both home and away against Coventry, Newcastle and Watford!

● Liverpool used a total of 20 players and of them only two – Jan Molby and John Wark – have never started a match!

● Mike Hooper deputised for Bruce Grobbelaar on two occasions during the run and kept clean sheets against both Arsenal and Charlton!

● Liverpool conceded more than one goal on only two occasions ... against Charlton on September 15 and Southampton on December 12!

● Liverpool won 24 of their 29 unbeaten games. The draws came against West Ham (twice), Norwich, Wimbledon and Manchester United!

● Liverpool were watched by a total of 980,235 'Match Facts' was 3.69 for the 29-game run. Satisfactory to good value every week!

● Liverpool were watched by a total of 980,235 people and, when Everton finally brought the run to an end in the 30th game at Goodison Park, it meant that 1,024,397 spectators had seen the 'Reds'!

● Liverpool's best home crowd was the 44,760 for the Merseyside 'derby' with Everton which they won 2-0. The lowest home crowd was 31,211 for the visit of Chelsea!

THE GOAL THAT SPARKED A RECORD CHASE ...

John Aldridge (third left) gets on the end of a John Barnes cross at Highbury to head past John Lukic and the 'Reds' are off and running with a 2-1 win against Arsenal.

... AND THE GOAL THAT ENDED IT

Below: After 29 long games, Wayne Clarke (partly hidden) fires the winner past Bruce Grobbelaar in the 14th minute of a tense Merseyside derby.

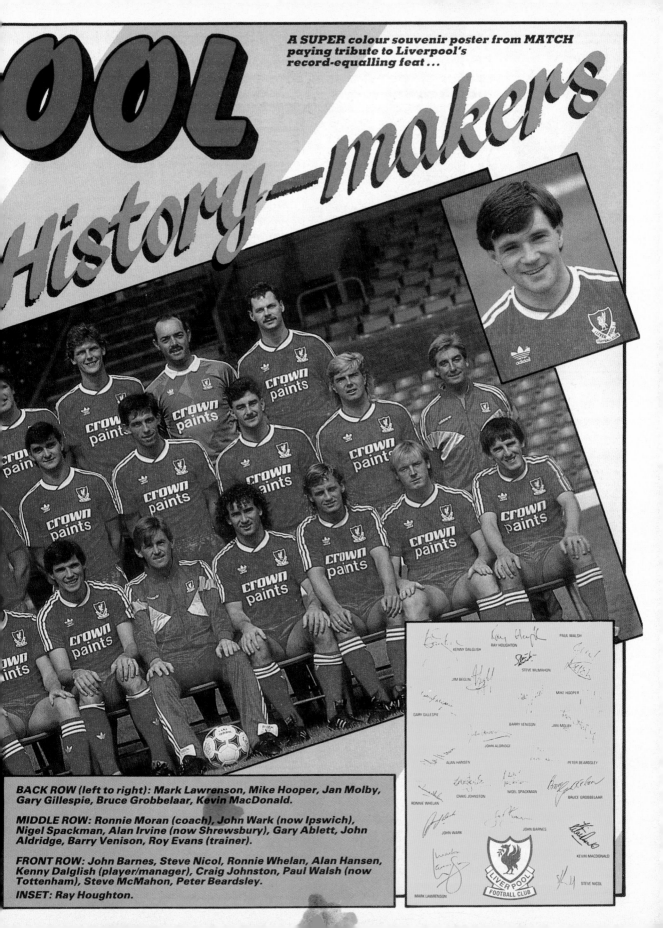

OOL

History-makers

A SUPER colour souvenir poster from MATCH paying tribute to Liverpool's record-equalling feat ...

BACK ROW (left to right): Mark Lawrenson, Mike Hooper, Jan Molby, Gary Gillespie, Bruce Grobbelaar, Kevin MacDonald.

MIDDLE ROW: Ronnie Moran (coach), John Wark (now Ipswich), Nigel Spackman, Alan Irvine (now Shrewsbury), Gary Ablett, John Aldridge, Barry Venison, Roy Evans (trainer).

FRONT ROW: John Barnes, Steve Nicol, Ronnie Whelan, Alan Hansen, Kenny Dalglish (player/manager), Craig Johnston, Paul Walsh (now Tottenham), Steve McMahon, Peter Beardsley.

INSET: Ray Houghton.

DON-FIRE

WIMBLEDON FIREWORKS SINK LIVERPOOL

The goal that won the Cup! Horror for goalkeeper Bruce Grobbelaar as the ball hits the net and Wimbledon's Lawrie Sanchez (arms raised) celebrates the header that beat red-hot favourites Liverpool.

PARTY!

PENALTY! *Wimbledon full-back Clive Goodyear is adjudged to have fouled John Aldridge as the Liverpool striker sprawls over his outstretched leg. But Dons' skipper Dave Beasant is equal to Aldridge's spot-kick, pushing the ball to safety to become the first goalkeeper to save a penalty in an FA Cup Final.*

GUL

RIGHT: Moment of despair for striker Igor Belanov as his penalty is saved by Holland 'keeper Hans Van Breukelen.

LEFT: Goalscorer Gullit collapses under the weight of congratulations from Dutch team-mates.

LIT-INED!

THE
88
BATTLE FOR EUROPE!

RUUD BOYS GIVE RUSSIA THE CHOP

TWO players who would walk into any side in the world blasted Holland to European Championship glory in Munich's Olympic Stadium on Saturday.

A double dose of Milan magic from AC Milan team-mates Ruud Gullit and Marco Van Basten did the damage — 'Gullit the bullet' powering in an unstoppable header for the opening goal and Van Basten sealing a 2-0 victory over the resilient Russians with one of the greatest goals ever seen.

That astonishing, narrow-angled volley put the mark of greatness on a player whose performances in Germany have eclipsed even those of Gullit himself.

Yet Van Basten, who savaged England with a stunning hat-trick and who flattened favourites West Germany with his Semi-Final winner, was not even picked for the opening group game!

Re-instated for the match against England, magic Marco unveiled the flair, ingenuity, pace and inspired finishing that put in question Gullit's top billing in a Holland team brimming with talent.

It was a talent even the tough and enterprising Russians could not prevent from overflowing and now the devastating Dutch will look forward to the 1990 World Cup with great optimism.

• The new England... Pages 20 and 21.
• The Dutch Destroyer... Pages 10 and 11.

ABOVE: Gullit's bullet! The dreadlocks fly as Ruud Gullit's header rockets over the head of Russian 'keeper Rinat Dasaev and into the net for Holland's first goal.

FULL NAME: Paul Ince.
BIRTHPLACE/DATE: October 21, 1967.
HEIGHT/WEIGHT: 5ft 11ins/11st 6lbs.
MARRIED: No, but I'm engaged to Clare.

WHAT ARE YOUR FAVOURITE ARTICLES OF CLOTHING? Jeans and T-shirt.
WHO IS YOUR MOST FAMOUS FRIEND OUTSIDE FOOTBALL? The boxer, Frank Bruno.
WHAT SUBJECT DID YOU HATE MOST AT SCHOOL AND WHY? Everything except PE!
WHAT WOULD YOU DO IF SOMEONE GAVE YOU £50,000 TODAY? Say thank you, and then put it straight in the bank.
WHAT IS YOUR CLAIM TO FAME OUTSIDE FOOTBALL? I once saved my brother from being hit by a car and got run over myself in the process.
HOW MANY 'O' LEVELS DID YOU GET? None.
WHO WOULD YOU MOST LIKE TO MEET AND WHY? Daley Thompson – because I admire his determination to stay at the top.
WHAT, IF ANYTHING, FRIGHTENS YOU? Insects.
WHAT WAS THE FIRST CAR YOU BOUGHT AND HOW MUCH DID IT COST? A Ford Escort 1300 for £3,500.
WHO ARE YOUR FAVOURITE POP STARS? Anyone who plays jazz funk.

Playing football is about the only way I could earn a living.
OUTSIDE FOOTBALL WHAT IS THE BIGGEST RISK YOU HAVE EVER TAKEN? Eating my fiancee's cooking!
DO YOU HAVE ANY HOBBIES? Playing snooker and golf, and collecting jazz funk records.
WHICH DAY OF THE WEEK DO YOU DISLIKE MOST AND WHY? Monday – I hate getting up for training in the morning.
IF YOU COULD BE A FLY ON THE WALL WHERE WOULD YOU MOST LIKE TO BE? In the manager's office on a Friday afternoon when he picks the team.
HAVE YOU EVER BEEN MISTAKEN FOR SOMEONE ELSE? My friends think I look like the boxer Sugar Ray Leonard.

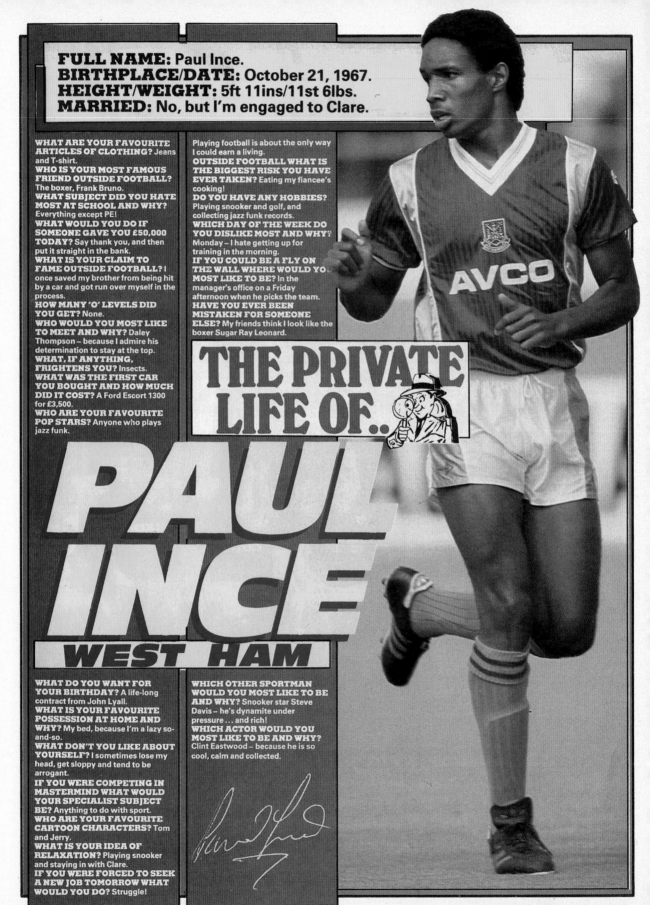

THE PRIVATE LIFE OF..

PAUL INCE

WEST HAM

WHAT DO YOU WANT FOR YOUR BIRTHDAY? A life-long contract from John Lyall.
WHAT IS YOUR FAVOURITE POSSESSION AT HOME AND WHY? My bed, because I'm a lazy so-and-so.
WHAT DON'T YOU LIKE ABOUT YOURSELF? I sometimes lose my head, get sloppy and tend to be arrogant.
IF YOU WERE COMPETING IN MASTERMIND WHAT WOULD YOUR SPECIALIST SUBJECT BE? Anything to do with sport.
WHO ARE YOUR FAVOURITE CARTOON CHARACTERS? Tom and Jerry.
WHAT IS YOUR IDEA OF RELAXATION? Playing snooker and staying in with Clare.
IF YOU WERE FORCED TO SEEK A NEW JOB TOMORROW WHAT WOULD YOU DO? Struggle!

WHICH OTHER SPORTMAN WOULD YOU MOST LIKE TO BE AND WHY? Snooker star Steve Davis – he's dynamite under pressure . . . and rich!
WHICH ACTOR WOULD YOU MOST LIKE TO BE AND WHY? Clint Eastwood – because he is so cool, calm and collected.

1988-89

Michael Thomas, Hillsborough
and Sutton stun Coventry.

1988-89

TONY'S MEGA MOVE!

August 6, 1988

Everton break the British transfer record to sign West Ham striker Tony Cottee for £2.2 million. The 23-year-old admits the move ends six months of sleepless nights and hopes it will get him into Bobby Robson's World Cup squad.

OSSIE OUSTED!

September 10, 1988

Ossie Ardiles, now 36 years old, is bitterly disappointed as he leaves Tottenham. Ex-Liverpool defender Mark Lawrenson reckons the title won't go to a London team due to the number of tough derbies. Arsenal have other ideas...

FESTIVE TREAT!

December 24, 1988

A startling 88% of MATCH readers want Glenn Hoddle to get an England recall, though he's played his final international. Brian McClair wants to get Viv Anderson a new body for Christmas 'after all the injuries he's had'.

CUP KINGS!

April 15, 1989

Nigel Clough scores twice on Father's Day to guide Nottingham Forest to their first major success in nine years. Clough Senior leaves Wembley before the League Cup is lifted, while Neil Webb hopes it's just the start of more success.

ANFIELD DRAMA!

June 3, 1989

Michael Thomas hits a stoppage-time winner at Anfield to win the title for Arsenal on the final day. Alan Smith says the look on the Liverpool players' faces will live with him forever. "You felt they'd lost a war," he tells MATCH.

MERSON BOWLED OVER!

TOP MARK

HUGHES GETS THE PLAYER...

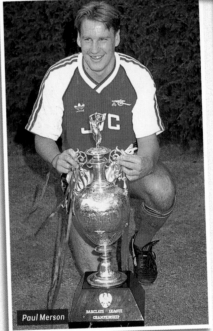

Paul Merson

Mark Hughes

⟫ STAR PLAYERS!

MARK HUGHES, Man. United: After spells with Barcelona and Bayern Munich, Hughes returned to Old Trafford in a club-record £1.8 million deal. Despite suffering a miserable season – finishing 11th in the league and failing in both cups – Sparky managed an impressive 16 goals.

PAUL MERSON, Arsenal: Merson was an established first-teamer when he was recognised in the PFA awards. Ripping up the right wing, Merse created the chances for Alan Smith and bagged ten goals as Arsenal pipped Liverpool to the title.

BEST KIT!

Crystal Palace home kit.

WORST KIT!

Aston Villa home kit.

» SEASON HIGHLIGHTS!

AUGUST: Ian Rush returns to Liverpool from Juventus in a £2.8 million deal.

SEPTEMBER: Arsenal's Paul Davis gets a nine-game ban and £3,000 fine after breaking the jaw of Southampton midfielder Glenn Cockerill.

OCTOBER: Brothers Danny, Rodney and Ray Wallace play for Southampton as they lose 2-1 to Sheffield Wednesday.

NOVEMBER: Norwich open up a seven-point lead at the top of Division One after beating Wimbledon 2-0 – their eighth win in 11 league games.

DECEMBER: Tottenham sign the biggest sponsorship deal in British football, agreeing a three-year, £1.3 million contract with Holsten.

JANUARY: Non-league Sutton produce the shock result of the FA Cup third round, beating 1987 winners Coventry 2-1.

FEBRUARY: Brian Clough is hit with a £5,000 fine and banned from the dugout for the rest of the season after hitting two pitch invaders.

MARCH: West Ham pay Celtic £1.25 million for former striker Frank McAvennie.

APRIL: 96 Liverpool fans lose their lives at Hillsborough after a crowd surge in their FA Cup semi with Nottingham Forest.

MAY: Liverpool win an emotionally-charged FA Cup final, beating rivals Everton 3-2, but lose the league title to a last-minute goal from Arsenal's Michael Thomas.

Clockwise from top: Cloughie is banned from the dugout, Robert Fleck and his team-mates finish fourth, Neil Webb and Nigel Clough score in the Littlewoods Cup final and Liverpool legend Ian Rush returns to Anfield after his forgetful spell with Juventus.

» RISING STARS!

DAVID PLATT: A year before winning the PFA Player Of The Year award, Aston Villa's dynamic attacking midfielder demonstrated his versatility by playing in all 38 of the club's league games, hitting the net seven times.

NIGEL CLOUGH: Displaying the skills in front of goal that his father showed in his playing days, Clough Junior was the top scorer in Nottingham Forest's successful Littlewoods Cup campaign, and hit 14 League goals as the club finished an impressive third in Division One.

» FINAL LEAGUE TABLES!

DIVISION ONE

	CLUB	P	W	D	L	F	A	GD	Pts
1	Arsenal	38	22	10	6	73	36	+37	76
2	Liverpool	38	22	10	6	65	28	+37	76
3	Nott'm Forest	38	17	13	8	64	43	+21	64
4	Norwich	38	17	11	10	48	45	+3	62
5	Derby	38	17	7	14	40	38	+2	58
6	Tottenham	38	15	12	11	60	46	+14	57
7	Coventry	38	14	13	11	47	42	+5	55
8	Everton	38	14	12	12	50	45	+5	54
9	QPR	38	14	11	13	43	37	+6	53
10	Millwall	38	14	11	13	47	52	-5	53
11	Man. United	38	13	12	13	45	35	+10	51
12	Wimbledon	38	14	9	15	50	46	+4	51
13	Southampton	38	10	15	13	52	66	-14	45
14	Charlton	38	10	12	16	44	58	-14	42
15	Sheff. Wed.	38	10	12	16	34	51	-17	42
16	Luton	38	10	11	17	42	52	-10	41
17	Aston Villa	38	9	13	16	45	56	-11	40
18	Middlesbrough	38	9	12	17	44	61	-17	39
19	West Ham	38	10	8	20	37	62	-25	38
20	Newcastle	38	7	10	21	32	63	-31	31

TOP SCORER: Alan Smith Arsenal, 23 goals

DIVISION TWO

	CLUB	P	W	D	L	F	A	GD	Pts
1	Chelsea	46	29	12	5	96	50	+46	99
2	Man. City	46	23	13	10	77	53	+24	82
3	Crystal Palace	46	23	12	11	71	49	+22	81
4	Watford	46	22	12	12	74	48	+26	78
5	Blackburn	46	22	11	13	74	59	+15	77
6	Swindon	46	20	16	10	68	53	+15	76
7	Barnsley	46	20	14	12	66	58	+8	74
8	Ipswich	46	22	7	17	71	61	+10	73
9	West Brom	46	18	18	10	65	41	+24	72
10	Leeds	46	17	16	13	59	50	+9	67
11	Sunderland	46	16	15	15	60	60	0	63
12	Bournemouth	46	18	8	20	53	62	-9	62
13	Stoke	46	15	14	17	57	72	-15	59
14	Bradford	46	13	17	16	52	59	-7	56
15	Leicester	46	13	16	17	56	63	-7	55
16	Oldham	46	11	21	14	75	72	+3	54
17	Oxford	46	14	12	20	62	70	-8	54
18	Plymouth	46	14	12	20	55	66	-11	54
19	Brighton	46	14	9	23	57	66	-9	51
20	Portsmouth	46	13	12	21	53	62	-9	51
21	Hull	46	11	14	21	52	68	-16	47
22	Shrewsbury	46	8	18	20	40	67	-27	42
23	Birmingham	46	8	11	27	31	76	-45	35
24	Walsall	46	5	16	25	41	80	-39	31

TOP SCORER: Keith Edwards Hull, 26 goals

DIVISION THREE

	CLUB	P	W	D	L	F	A	GD	Pts
1	Wolves	46	26	14	6	96	49	+47	92
2	Sheff. United	46	25	9	12	93	54	+39	84
3	Port Vale	46	24	12	10	78	48	+30	84
4	Fulham	46	22	9	15	69	67	+2	75
5	Bristol Rovers	46	19	17	10	67	51	+16	74
6	Preston	46	19	15	12	79	60	+19	72
7	Brentford	46	18	14	14	66	61	+5	68
8	Chester	46	19	11	16	64	61	+3	68
9	Notts County	46	18	13	15	64	54	+10	67
10	Bolton	46	16	16	14	58	54	+4	64
11	Bristol City	46	18	9	19	53	55	-2	63
12	Swansea	46	15	16	15	51	53	-2	61
13	Bury	46	16	13	17	55	67	-12	61
14	Huddersfield	46	17	9	20	63	73	-10	60
15	Mansfield	46	14	17	15	48	52	-4	59
16	Cardiff	46	14	15	17	44	56	-12	57
17	Wigan	46	14	14	18	55	53	+2	56
18	Reading	46	15	11	20	68	72	-4	56
19	Blackpool	46	14	12	20	56	59	-3	54
20	Northampton	46	16	6	24	66	76	-10	54
21	Southend	46	13	15	18	56	75	-19	54
22	Chesterfield	46	14	7	25	51	86	-35	49
23	Gillingham	46	12	4	30	47	81	-34	40
24	Aldershot	46	8	13	25	48	78	-30	37

TOP SCORER: Steve Bull Wolves, 37 goals

DIVISION FOUR

	CLUB	P	W	D	L	F	A	GD	Pts
1	Rotherham	46	22	16	8	76	35	+41	82
2	Tranmere	46	21	17	8	62	43	+19	80
3	Crewe	46	21	15	10	67	48	+19	78
4	Scunthorpe	46	21	14	11	77	57	+20	77
5	Scarborough	46	21	14	11	67	52	+15	77
6	Leyton Orient	46	21	12	13	86	50	+36	75
7	Wrexham	46	19	14	13	77	63	+14	71
8	Cambridge	46	18	14	14	71	62	+9	68
9	Grimsby	46	17	15	14	65	59	+6	66
10	Lincoln	46	18	10	18	64	60	+4	64
11	York	46	17	13	16	62	63	-1	64
12	Carlisle	46	15	15	16	53	52	+1	60
13	Exeter	46	18	6	22	65	68	-3	60
14	Torquay	46	17	8	21	45	60	-15	59
15	Hereford	46	14	16	16	66	72	-6	58
16	Burnley	46	14	13	19	52	61	-9	55
17	Peterborough	46	14	12	20	52	74	-22	54
18	Rochdale	46	13	14	19	56	82	-26	53
19	Hartlepool	46	14	10	22	50	78	-28	52
20	Stockport	46	13	15	18	54	52	+2	51
21	Halifax	46	13	11	22	69	75	-6	50
22	Colchester	46	14	7	25	60	78	-18	50
23	Doncaster	46	13	10	23	49	78	-29	49
24	Darlington	46	8	18	20	53	76	-23	42

TOP SCORER: Phil Stant Hereford, 28 goals

SUTTON'S

VAUXHALL Conference minnows Sutton United pulled off the shock of the Third Round with their sensational 2-1 victory over former holders Coventry, while at Crewe Graham Taylor's Aston Villa had the fright of their lives as the Fourth Division outfit took a 2-0 lead, only to be beaten 3-2 in a second half comeback. MATCH was at both games to bring you these exclusive pictures. Pictures: Phil Bagnall and Paul Marriott.

Editor: Melvyn Bagnall
News Editor: Paul Stratton
Reporters:
Howard Wheatcroft, Ray Ryan, Paul Smith
Production Editor: Mick Weavers
Design: Wayne Kirk
Photographer: Philip Bagnall
Editor's secretary: Kate Harrison
Advertisement Manager: Brian Reacher
Advertisement Assistant: Mike Wells
Product Manager: Denis Stapleton
Publisher: Ken Gill
Premium Sales Manager: Neil Pitcher

Vol. 10   No. 18

MATCH

Editorial: Stirling House, Bretton, Peterborough PE3 8DJ. Tel: 0733 260333/264666
Advertising and Marketing: Bretton Court, Bretton, Peterborough PE3 8DZ. Tel: 0733 264666

Reader Offers: P.O. Box 136, Peterborough PE2 0XW. Tel: 0733 237111
Circulation and Back Issues: Frontline, Park House, 117 Park Road, Peterborough PE1 2TR. Tel: 0733 555161
Subscriptions: P.O. Box 500, Leicester LE99 0AA. Orderline 0858 410888
Mono origination: Typefont Ltd
Colour origination: Lumarcolour Ltd
Printing: Chase Web, Barnstaple
© EMAP Pursuit Publishing Ltd 1989 Registered at the Post Office as a newspaper

STUNNERS!

CUP JOY for Sutton 'keeper Trevor Roffey as the final whistle signals the biggest shock of the Third Round.

Above: THE WINNER! Bricklayer Matthew Hanlan thumps the ball past despairing Coventry 'keeper Steve Ogrizovic to clinch a sensational Cup victory for Sutton.
Left: FIRST BLOOD to Sutton as Tony Rains (second left) flashes a header into the Coventry net.

Above: CREWE-SING! Jubilation for the Fourth Division hopefuls after Mark Gardiner's fifth minute goal.
Left: Former Crewe player David Platt (third from right) begins the Villa revival with his second half strike.

MATCH FA CUP EXCLUSIVE

THE SCARVES OF SORROW

A HANDFUL of Liverpool scarves fluttered on a crush barrier at the Leppings Lane end of a deserted Hillsborough summing up a day in British football that will live long after winners and losers are nothing more than an entry in the record books.

The scarves belonged to supporters who had left Merseyside in the bright sunshine of a perfect Spring day to witness one of the season's great spectacles – the FA Cup Semi-Final between Liverpool and Nottingham Forest.

Instead they were caught up in a tragedy, the memory of which will stay with those involved forever.

Tribute

The red and white colours worn so proudly in the hours leading up to kick-off were left to serve as a tribute to the people who lost their lives.

They died in an horrific crush at the front of the stand minutes before the start as chaos broke out when scores of latecomers flooded on to the already jammed terraces.

Almost exactly 13 years ago, I stood on the very same spot as a Manchester United fan watching a Semi-Final against Derby. I didn't enjoy that afternoon because of the cramped conditions, but nothing could have prepared me for what unfolded at the start of one of the season's most eagerly-awaited fixtures.

The game was just beginning to settle down when the first of the fans climbed over the high blue perimeter fencing, but

MATCH reporter Howard Wheatcroft pays his own tribute to a day neither he nor football will ever forget . . .

play continued and it seemed the police would sort out the problem and it would soon be business as usual.

But more and more fans began to scramble over, the police clambered up from the playing side hoping to help people escape while at the same time attempting to ease the crush with shouts and desperate hand gestures.

Suddenly, six minutes into the match, the players were led off with huge numbers of people spilling onto the pitch. Some of those people were lying motionless with desperate friends and relatives huddled round them.

More and more police were flooding into the ground and making their way towards the Liverpool end, but at least 80 per cent of the 53,000 crowd still had no idea just how serious the problem was.

Then an ambulance began snaking its way up the side of the pitch as fast as the milling fans would allow and, combined with the frenzied action immediately behind the goal, the awful depth of the tragedy began to sink in.

But by now it was hard to do anything but stare in utter disbelief at the events just a few hundred yards away behind the goal Forest should have been attacking.

Half of you wanted to watch the scenes, the other half to turn your back in the vain hope it might go away.

And so many of the other fans watching from the stand – myself included – knew that at another time and at another place it could easily have been them standing behind that goal.

By now, advertising hoardings were being ripped down and turned into makeshift stretchers – many of them carried away by fans to the far corner of the ground and the waiting ambulances.

Firemen were on the scene but at times the first aid crews didn't seem to know which way to turn. The images of Heysel came flooding back.

There was still no official news over the tannoy about what had happened, but word was beginning to filter out that there might have been deaths – four being the first figure.

Some 70 minutes after play had been stopped it was announced the game was being abandoned, but fans were asked to stay inside the ground to help ambulances get to and from hospital.

Most stayed as requested and it was only when they got into cars and coaches and listened to the radio that they realised the extent of the disaster.

As they wound their silent way home, they left behind a deserted stadium that must have looked much as it did before kick-off.

But as the setting afternoon sun illuminated the blue and white paint, bare concrete and those lonely red and white scarves, the realisation dawned that Hillsborough, the FA Cup – and indeed football – will never be quite the same.

Three abandoned police helmets lay strewn in the corner of the Hillsborough pitch in symbolic salute to the efforts of the emergency services on the fateful day of April 15, 1989 – a picture that will forever live in the memory of football fans the world over.

It's there! With just four minutes on the clock, John Aldridge races on to a McMahon pass to fire a great shot past Neville Southall and give Liverpool the perfect start.

BRING ON THE

NOW KENNY'S CUP

Above: Last gasp! With the red ribbons about to be tied to the FA Cup and Everton seemingly beaten, a goalmouth scramble ends with Stuart McCall stabbing the ball home to make the score 1-1 with just a minute of normal time remaining. Tony Cottee (left) is clearly off-side but the goal stands.

Stop that! Ian Rush (14) fires an unstoppable shot into the Everton net after turning his marker Kevin Ratcliffe and Liverpool are back in the lead at 2-1.

GUNNERS!
HEROES LOOK TO THE LEAGUE

LIVERPOOL now stand just 90 minutes away from the elusive 'double double' – their meeting with Championship rivals Arsenal at Anfield on Friday providing a dramatic finish to a season full of drama.

And if the 'Gunners' needed any reminding of the fire power which threatens Cockney hopes of a title-winning knees-up it was there for all to see as Liverpool successfully completed the first leg of their two-trophy chase with victory over Everton in Saturday's FA Cup Final.

Twice the 'Toffees' clawed themselves back into the match when all seemed lost. But not for the first time it was Ian Rush who proved the thorn in their side with two sweetly taken extra-time goals which put all the problems of his troublesome first season at Anfield behind him.

MATCH captures the excitement of one of Wembley's most thrilling encounters in super colour...

LAST GASP

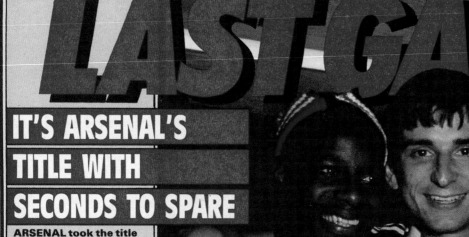

IT'S ARSENAL'S TITLE WITH SECONDS TO SPARE

ARSENAL took the title back to London for the first time in 18 long years following what was surely the most dramatic finale to a League season ever witnessed.

They went to Liverpool's Anfield fortress for the final match of the First Division campaign needing what most people believed was an impossible result – victory by at least two clear goals.

And against all the odds they did it with just seconds to spare.

'The look on the Liverpool players' faces will live with me forever'
— Kevin Richardson

❝ WHEN Michael Thomas scored our second goal I felt like my whole inside had dropped out.

And the look on the faces of the Liverpool players will live with me forever.

They just fell to the ground like casualties on a battle-field.

But 15 minutes earlier I thought we had blown it.

I played a ball through to Michael and with only Bruce Grobbelaar to beat he shot straight at the Liverpool 'keeper.

I remember thinking we'd never get another chance like that but thank God I was wrong.

Everybody wrote us off before the game especially in view of the way Liverpool had been playing in the closing stages of the season.

However we knew we could win and as the game approached the half-hour mark, you could tell our lads were growing in confidence but I must admit we left it a bit late. ❞

Dressing room delight! Arsenal goalscorers Michael Thomas and Alan Smith celebrate with the League Championship trophy following the 'Gunners' dramatic Anfield victory.

'I'M STILL IN DREAMLAND'
— ALAN SMITH

❝ ANY minute now I'm expecting to awake from a dream because it still hasn't hit home that Arsenal are the new League Champions!

As we made the long trip to Anfield we were given no chance of achieving anything and I can't tell you what it feels like to have proved so many people wrong. It seemed we were the only ones with any confidence in our ability and I sensed even our own supporters felt we'd left it too late.

Obviously scoring a goal makes that winning feeling even better although once I'd headed Kevin Richardson's cross I wondered whether the ball would ever cross the line!

Once we had our noses in front, however, I sensed we had the ability to go on and win the game although we did leave it a bit late and even when Michael Thomas scored I was convinced the referee would disallow it for some reason or another.

But what can you say about Liverpool and how can you compensate being seconds away from retaining the League title only to have it snatched from you in such dramatic fashion.

The look on their faces when we scored our second frightened me. Many of them were on their knees and you felt they'd lost a war! ❞

'GUNNERS'!

The ball is on its way past Bruce Grobbelaar from the boot of Michael Thomas and the title is on its way to Highbury.

● SUPER COLOUR ARSENAL SOUVENIR POSTER – SEE CENTRE PAGES!

Alan Smith powers home his header for Arsenal's first goal.

THE STEVE McMAHON COLUMN

❝I'M absolutely devastated! Weeks after looking like we were going to retain our League crown we blew it at the last hurdle and what makes matters worse is that during the whole match against the 'Gunners', Bruce Grobbelaar didn't have a single save to make! Arsenal had two attacks and scored from them both.

But that's the way football tends to go and we can't begrudge George Graham's side the title. Anyone who wins the Championship over 38 games deserves it and no-one can say it was a fluke.

Despite losing the title in the last game of the season, we have still had a good year. After all, we've won the FA Cup and not many sides can say they've achieved that!

But obviously we're disappointed that we didn't achieve that elusive 'double double' and at the end of the day, I suppose we played too many crucial games in a short time and it took its toll on us.

After weeks of trying to catch Arsenal in the Championship race we were shattered and the last match of the season was like trying to squeeze blood from a stone.

I'm not trying to make excuses, but while we were jaded the 'Gunners' were very fresh after having an easier run-in compared to us.

The boss had one or two strong words to say to the lads in the dressing room afterwards and the disappointment of May 26 will live with me forever.❞

CANNON-BULL!

TON-UP STEVE SHOOTS WOLVES TO PROMOTION

STEVE BULL set up Wolves' glorious return to the Second Division with his own brand of May Day celebrations.

Not only did his double strike in the 2-0 home win over Bristol City re-inforce the inevitable return of the Molineux side to the higher grade but, in notching his 48th goal of this season, he became the first player since the war to hit 100 in just two terms, having rattled home 52 in all competitions as the Wanderers stormed out of Divison Four in 1987-88.

BULLY'S TON OF GOALS

	Lge	FA Cup	Lge Cup	Others	Total
Season 1987-88 (Division Four)	34	3	3	12	52
Season 1988-89 (Division Three)	35	–	2	11	48

● Up to and including games played on May 1, 1989.

1989-90

*Gazza's tears, Roger Milla
and Ian Wright.*

1989-90

THE NEW SPUR!

July 1, 1989

"Everton came in for me and Monaco would have been the choice if it was down to money, but my mind was made up," says Gary Lineker as he joins England team-mates Paul Gascoigne and Chris Waddle at Tottenham.

CUP SPECIAL!

April 28, 1990

David Platt casts his eye over the men to watch in the Littlewoods Cup final. Des Walker and Steve Hodge are the pick of the Nottingham Forest side, while Mike Milligan and Rick Holden are Oldham's star players.

MILLA MAGIC!

June 30, 1990

Cameroon's 38-year-old striker Roger Milla insists the Indomitable Lions can win the World Cup. Amazingly, Milla shouldn't even be at the Finals – he was only reinstated after Paul Biya, the country's President, intervened.

BUTCHER'S DREAM!

July 7, 1990

Stand-in England skipper Terry Butcher reveals a recurring dream he has of lifting the World Cup. Carlos Valderrama wins the award for the worst haircut of the tournament. MATCH likens him to a 'badly groomed mop'.

GERMAN JOY!

July 14, 1990

In the aftermath of Argentina's World Cup final defeat, Diego Maradona says he wants to retire from international football. Franz Beckenbauer is only the second man to play and manage a World Cup-winning side.

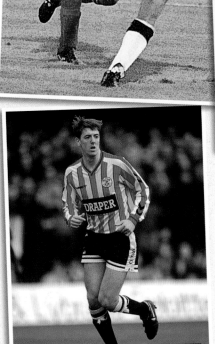

Platt stuns Belgium

David Platt

>> STAR PLAYERS!

DAVID PLATT, Aston Villa:
The former Man. United trainee made his name with Crewe before moving to Aston Villa. He scored 21 goals as The Villans finished second and ended the season in Bobby Robson's World Cup squad.

MATT LE TISSIER, Southampton:
The Saints would have been a very ordinary team without this man. Playing behind the frontmen, Le Tissier netted 24 goals, floating in from the wing to punish any gaps left by defenders.

Matt Le Tissier

BEST KIT!

West Germany's World Cup kit.

WORST KIT!

Liverpool's grey away kit.

» SEASON HIGHLIGHTS!

JULY: Spurs and England winger Chris Waddle joins French giants Marseille for a record £4.25 million.

AUGUST: Property investor Michael Knighton juggles a ball on the Old Trafford pitch, stating his £20 million bid for Man. United is genuine.

SEPTEMBER: Liverpool thrash Crystal Palace 9-0, Division One's biggest win in 26 years.

OCTOBER: England qualify for the 1990 World Cup following a goalless draw against Poland.

NOVEMBER: Nigel Martyn is Britain's first £1 million keeper, moving from Bristol Rovers to Crystal Palace.

DECEMBER: South African-born QPR striker Roy Wegerle turns down England and pledges his future to the USA.

JANUARY: Lord Taylor's Hillsborough report rules that all Division One football stadia must be all-seater by 1999.

FEBRUARY: Man. United end a run of 11 league games without a win by beating Millwall 2-1.

MARCH: FIFA tell all referees that any tackles from behind are red card offences.

APRIL: Crystal Palace gain revenge for their 9-0 defeat at Liverpool by beating The Reds 4-3 in the FA Cup semi-final.

MAY: Juventus set a new world record by paying Fiorentina £7.7 million for Roberto Baggio.

JUNE: An Andreas Brehme penalty wins the World Cup for West Germany.

Paul Ince Man. United

Clockwise from top: The days look numbered for Man. United manager Alex Ferguson, MATCH asks readers to give their verdict on Lord Taylor's Hillsborough report, English clubs are back in Europe after five years and West Ham's Paul Ince joins Man. United.

» RISING STARS!

NIGEL MARTYN: "We're selling him on the cheap," says Bristol Rovers boss Gerry Francis as Martyn becomes Britain's first £1 million keeper. Perry Suckling steps aside as Martyn makes the No.1 jersey his own for the next seven seasons.

DAVID SEAMAN: Martyn's transfer record doesn't last long as the QPR shot-stopper joins Arsenal for £1.3 million. He's called up to England's World Cup squad, but pulls out with a thumb injury.

» FINAL LEAGUE TABLES!

DIVISION ONE

	CLUB	P	W	D	L	F	A	GD	Pts
1	Liverpool	38	23	10	5	78	37	+41	79
2	Aston Villa	38	21	7	10	57	38	+19	70
3	Tottenham	38	19	6	13	59	47	+12	63
4	Arsenal	38	18	8	12	54	38	+16	62
5	Chelsea	38	16	12	10	58	50	+8	60
6	Everton	38	17	8	13	57	46	+11	59
7	Southampton	38	15	10	13	71	63	+8	55
8	Wimbledon	38	13	16	9	47	40	+7	55
9	Nott'm Forest	38	15	9	14	55	47	+8	54
10	Norwich	38	13	14	11	44	42	+2	53
11	QPR	38	13	11	14	45	44	+1	50
12	Coventry	38	14	7	17	39	59	-20	49
13	Man. United	38	13	9	16	46	47	-1	48
14	Man. City	38	12	12	14	43	52	-9	48
15	Crystal Palace	38	13	9	16	42	66	-24	48
16	Derby	38	13	7	18	43	40	+3	46
17	Luton	38	10	13	15	43	57	-14	43
18	Sheff. Wed.	38	11	10	17	35	51	-16	43
19	Charlton	38	7	9	22	31	57	-26	30
20	Millwall	38	5	11	22	39	65	-26	26

TOP SCORER: Gary Lineker Tottenham, 24 goals

DIVISION TWO

	CLUB	P	W	D	L	F	A	GD	Pts
1	Leeds	46	24	13	9	79	52	+27	85
2	Sheff. United	46	24	13	9	78	58	+20	85
3	Newcastle	46	22	14	10	80	55	+25	80
4	Swindon	46	20	14	12	79	59	+20	74
5	Blackburn	46	19	17	10	74	59	+15	74
6	Sunderland	46	20	14	12	70	64	+6	74
7	West Ham	46	20	12	14	80	57	+23	72
8	Oldham	46	19	14	13	70	57	+13	71
9	Ipswich	46	19	12	15	67	66	+1	69
10	Wolves	46	18	13	15	67	60	+7	67
11	Port Vale	46	15	16	15	62	57	+5	61
12	Portsmouth	46	15	16	15	62	65	-3	61
13	Leicester	46	15	14	17	67	79	-12	59
14	Hull	46	14	16	16	58	65	-7	58
15	Watford	46	14	17	15	58	60	-2	57
16	Plymouth	46	14	13	19	58	63	-5	55
17	Oxford	46	15	9	22	57	66	-9	54
18	Brighton	46	15	9	22	56	72	-16	54
19	Barnsley	46	13	15	18	49	71	-22	54
20	West Brom	46	12	15	19	67	71	-4	51
21	Middlesbrough	46	13	11	22	52	63	-11	50
22	Bournemouth	46	12	12	22	57	76	-19	48
23	Bradford	46	9	14	23	44	68	-24	41
24	Stoke	46	6	19	21	35	63	-28	37

TOP SCORER: Micky Quinn Newcastle, 32 goals

DIVISION THREE

	CLUB	P	W	D	L	F	A	GD	Pts
1	Bristol Rovers	46	26	15	5	71	35	+36	93
2	Bristol City	46	27	10	9	76	40	+36	91
3	Notts County	46	25	12	9	73	53	+20	87
4	Tranmere	46	23	11	12	86	49	+37	80
5	Bury	46	21	11	14	70	49	+21	74
6	Bolton	46	18	15	13	59	48	+11	69
7	Birmingham	46	18	12	16	60	59	+1	66
8	Huddersfield	46	17	14	15	61	62	-1	65
9	Rotherham	46	17	13	16	71	62	+9	64
10	Reading	46	15	19	12	57	53	+4	64
11	Shrewsbury	46	16	15	15	59	54	+5	63
12	Crewe	46	15	17	14	56	53	+3	62
13	Brentford	46	18	7	21	66	66	0	61
14	Leyton Orient	46	16	10	20	52	56	-4	58
15	Mansfield	46	16	7	23	50	65	-15	55
16	Chester	46	13	15	18	43	55	-12	54
17	Swansea	46	14	12	20	45	63	-18	54
18	Wigan	46	13	14	19	48	64	-16	53
19	Preston	46	14	10	22	65	79	-14	52
20	Fulham	46	12	15	19	55	66	-11	51
21	Cardiff	46	12	14	20	51	70	-19	50
22	Northampton	46	11	14	21	51	68	-17	47
23	Blackpool	46	10	16	20	49	73	-24	46
24	Walsall	46	9	14	23	40	72	-32	41

TOP SCORER: Bob Taylor Bristol City, 27 goals

DIVISION FOUR

	CLUB	P	W	D	L	F	A	GD	Pts
1	Exeter	46	28	5	13	83	48	+35	89
2	Grimsby	46	22	13	11	70	47	+23	79
3	Southend	46	22	9	15	61	48	+13	75
4	Stockport	46	21	11	14	68	62	+6	74
5	Maidstone	46	22	7	17	77	61	+16	73
6	Cambridge	46	21	10	15	76	66	+10	73
7	Chesterfield	46	19	14	13	63	50	+13	71
8	Carlisle	46	21	8	17	61	60	+1	71
9	Peterborough	46	17	17	12	59	46	+13	68
10	Lincoln	46	18	14	14	48	48	0	68
11	Scunthorpe	46	17	15	14	69	54	+15	66
12	Rochdale	46	20	6	20	52	55	-3	66
13	York	46	16	16	14	55	53	+2	64
14	Gillingham	46	17	11	18	46	48	-2	62
15	Torquay	46	15	12	19	53	66	-13	57
16	Burnley	46	14	14	18	45	55	-10	56
17	Hereford	46	15	10	21	56	62	-6	55
18	Scarborough	46	15	10	21	60	73	-13	55
19	Hartlepool	46	15	10	21	66	88	-22	55
20	Doncaster	46	14	9	23	53	60	-7	51
21	Wrexham	46	13	12	21	51	67	-16	51
22	Aldershot	46	12	14	20	49	69	-20	50
23	Halifax	46	12	13	21	57	65	-8	49
24	Colchester	46	11	10	25	48	75	-27	43

TOP SCORER: Brett Angell Stockport, 23 goals

GET NEXT WEEK'S MATCH FOR THE BEST IN COLOUR PICTURES FROM THE FA CUP FINAL REPLAY!

Chaos in the United goalmouth as the combined efforts of Steve Bruce and Jim Leighton fail to keep out the looping header from Gary O'Reilly (centre).

WHEN Crystal Palace boss Steve Coppell sent on Ian Wright in the 69th minute he told him he could go out and win the Cup . . . and he so nearly succeeded.

With virtually his first touch he brilliantly beat off the challenge of two United players to make the score 2-2 when the game appeared to be slipping away from the London side.

And then he popped up at the other end in the second minute of extra-time to score what everyone thought would be the Wembley winner until Mark Hughes saved United's blushes and took the game to a replay.

WRI

The ball crashes into the United net following a great solo run by Ian Wright (out of picture).

Take that! Jim Leighton is powerless as Ian Wright flies in at the far post to crash home his second.

Palace pile! Celebration time following Ian Wright's brilliant first goal.

SUPER-SUB IAN BOUNCES
BACK WITH A WEMBLEY DOUBLE

GHT ON CUE!

INSIDE YOUR POSTER-PACKED MATCH

Vinny Jones — One of the Leeds' top men this season. Join him and his team on pages 17 and 24.

PRIVATE LIFE!
Tony Dorigo reveals all — Page 7.

FREE COMPETITION!
Win a Mace Sports Scholarship — Page 9.

WINNER WADDLE!
Chris's French joy — Pages 10 and 11.

WIN VIDEOS!
80 up for grabs — Page 12.

TEAM GROUP
Man. Utd in colour — Pages 16 and 25.

POSTER EXTRA!
Including Champions Leeds — Pages 17-24.

SUDDEN – DEATH SOCCER!
Play-off previews — Pages 38 and 39.

Editor: Paul Stratton ● **Design:** Wayne Kirk ● **Sub Editors:** Fiona Alexander, Nick Wood ● **Reporters:** Paul Smith, Nick Gibbs ● **Photographer:** Philip Bagnall ● **Editor's secretary:** Susan Peat ● **Advertisement Manager:** Nita Brett ● **Assistant Ad. Manager:** Wendy Toms ● **Classified advertising/Club shop:** Duncan Gibb ● **Production Assistant:** Rebecca Johnson ● **Publishing Director:** Ken Gill ● **Product Manager:** Alison Leventon.

Editorial: Bretton Court, Bretton, Peterborough PE3 8DZ. Tel: 0733 260333/264666.
Advertising and Marketing: Bretton Court, Bretton, Peterborough PE3 8DZ. Tel: 0733 264666.
Circulation: Frontline, Park House, 117 Park Road, Peterborough PE1 2TR. Tel: 0733 555161.
Subscriptions: P.O. Box 500, Leicester LE99 0AA. Tel: 0858 410510 (enquiries); 0858 410888 (orderline ansaphone).
Back issues: P. O. Box 500, Leicester LE99 0AA. Tel: 0858 410510.
Mono Origination: Total Typesetters Ltd.
Colour Origination: Lumarcolour Ltd.
Printing: Chase Web Ltd, St Ives plc.
© EMAP Pursuit Publishing Ltd 1990.
Registered at the Post Office as a newspaper.

VOLUME 11	No. 34

FRONT COVER PIC: Victorious United captain Bryan Robson holds aloft the FA Cup.

FA CUP FINAL REPLAY SPECIAL

SIX PAGES of Wembley coverage starts here as we bring you the REAL story behind United hero Lee Martin plus pictures of the night he'll never forget . . .
● STORIES: Paul Smith.
● PICTURES: Philip Bagnall/ Allsport.

WEMB~

Lee Martin goes past Palace's Andy Gray before firing the ball into the net for the only goal of the game.

EE WONDER!

Hero of the night
Lee Martin raises
the FA Cup high
over his head.

MARTIN'S FIRST GOAL WINS THE CUP FOR UNITED

LEE MARTIN struck the first and most important goal of his career, to emerge as the unlikely hero on a Wembley night of high emotions.

The rookie defender, a former YTS player who didn't cost United a penny, upstaged his £13 million colleagues with the only goal of the game.

He latched onto Neil Webb's superb through ball and showed all the poise of a seasoned marksman, crashing the ball home from ten yards in the 60th minute.

"The record books will say it's the second goal of my career but as far as I'm concerned it's my first," said the ecstatic 22-year-old.

"I was credited with a League goal at Upton Park last season but although I had the initial shot it was a West Ham player who put the ball in the net.

"No-one is taking this one away from me however! My head is in the clouds and I don't want to come down."

Martin admits he was a reluctant hero and had gone into the game more concerned about suffering with cramp.

"The Semi-Final and Final both went to extra-time and each time I collapsed with cramp in both legs.

"I never dreamed I would emerge a goal hero, but I'm glad I did because it saved my poor legs from suffering again!".

Another man to emerge as an unlikely hero was on-loan goalkeeper Les Sealey.

Alex Ferguson sensationally axed Jim Leighton from the side minutes before the kick-off and as a result his future at the club must be in doubt.

Ferguson, collecting his first piece of silverware in 3½ years at Old Trafford, admitted it was the biggest gamble of his managerial career.

But Sealey reinforced the manager's decision with a succession of brilliant saves.

After the final whistle however, Sealey made his way over to Leighton and presented the Scottish 'keeper with his medal — a gesture described by Ferguson as 'typical of the man'.

- MORE GREAT COLOUR PICTURES AND STORIES — PAGES 4 & 5.
- MANCHESTER UNITED TEAM GROUP — PAGES 16 & 25.

'Supersub' David Platt
celebrates his last-gasp winner
against Belgium.

PLATT'S MAG

At last the ball is in the back of
the net! David Platt had put
England in the Quarter-Finals of
the World Cup.

Enzo Scifo's shot rebounds off the post to deny Belgium the lead and possible victory.

SECOND PHASE
SPECIAL

THERE were less than 60 seconds left on the clock when 'Supersub' David Platt latched onto an inch-perfect Paul Gascoigne free-kick and turned to volley England into the World Cup Quarter-Finals with a sensational strike.

Here MATCH brings you all the best action from England's nail-biting Second Phase clash with Belgium.

Euphoric Mark Wright (14), Steve Bull (centre) and Stuart Pearce (right) congratulate David Platt (hidden) on his sensational turn-and-volley strike.

MY MAGIC MOMENT

❛ Paul Gascoigne knocked a good free-kick in and I just hooked it round. It was nice to score for Bryan Robson because we were all trying for him. For me personally it was brilliant — the most wonderful moment of my career — ENGLAND GOALSCORER DAVID PLATT. ❜

ENGLAND'S World Cup dream finally died at the hands of their old adversaries from West Germany, but like Jack Charlton's Ireland before them, they waved farewell to 'Italia '90' with their heads held high.

For shining star Paul Gascoigne there were only tears for souvenirs — a cruel second booking robbing him of the chance of a possible Final place.

In the end his dream would have been denied anyway — England's failure from the spot seeing West Germany through in yet another dramatic penalty shoot-out.

But 'Gazza' will be remembered for so much more as he came of age to prove he has the skills to match his comedy capers. England's 'Clown Prince' was just a bit special . . .

'GAZZA' CRIES AS A DREAM DIES

TEARS OF A

WORLD CUP SEMI-FINAL ACTION S

Hope and glory! Gary Lineker slides the ball into the German net to equalise Andreas Brehme's deflected opener, but the joy was to be short-lived as Franz Beckenbauer's side earned their Final place in the cruellest possible way.

The final farewell. A sad Paul Gascoigne wipes away the tears after a cruel second booking robbed him of the chance of any further participation . . . and robbed 'Italia '90' of a shining star.

CLOWN!

CIAL!

West German joy after Chris Waddle's penalty miss had cost England their place in the Final.

Proud in defeat. The look on Terry Butcher's face says it all as the England skipper salutes the travelling band of fans who saw their heroes come so close to World Cup glory.

inside your World Cup

MATCH

TARGET MEN!

The hottest properties in the world — Pages 6 and 7.

STUART PEARCE

Colour poster. Page 9.

TEARS OF A CLOWN

England Semi-Final special — Pages 10 and 11.

FUN OF THE CUP!

Colour picture special — Pages 18 and 31.

THEY DID US PROUD

England souvenir — Page 19.

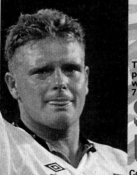

Paul Gascoigne — waving farewell to the World Cup.

● **Editor:** Paul Stratton ● **Design:** Wayne Kirk
● **Sub Editors:** Fiona Alexander, Nick Wood
● **Reporters:** Paul Smith, Nick Gibbs
● **Photographer:** Philip Bagnall ● **Editor's secretary:** Susan Peat ● **Advertisement Manager:** Nita Brett ● **Assistant Ad. Manager:** Wendy Toms ● **Classified advertising/Club shop:** Duncan Gibb ● **Production Assistant:** Rebecca Johnson ● **Publishing Director:** Ken Gill ● **Product Manager:** Alison Leventon.

Editorial: Bretton Court, Bretton, Peterborough PE3 8DZ.
Tel: 0733 260333/264666.
Advertising and Marketing: Bretton Court, Bretton, Peterborough PE3 8DZ. Tel: 0733 264666.
Circulation: Frontline, Park House, 117 Park Road, Peterborough PE1 2TR. Tel: 0733 555161.
Subscriptions: P.O. Box 500, Leicester LE99 0AA. Tel: 0858 410510 (enquiries): 0858 410888 (orderline ansaphone).
Back issues: P. O. Box 500, Leicester LE99 0AA. Tel: 0858 410510.
Mono Origination: Total Typesetters Ltd.
Colour Origination: Lumarcolour Ltd.
Printing: Chase Web Ltd, St Ives plc.
© EMAP Pursuit Publishing Ltd 1990.
Registered at the Post Office as a newspaper.

VOLUME II	No. 41

FRONT COVER PICTURE: Jürgen Kohler celebrates in style with the World Cup. Pictures; Allsport.

ON TOP O

ARGENTINA'S luck finally ran out as West Germany proved worthy winners of the 14th World Cup in Rome on Sunday.

But while the Germans had all the play, it still took a penalty to separate the two teams as they played out the finale to a competition dominated by spot-kicks.

MATCH brings you the best in colour action from the Italia '90 Final and over the page we spotlight the contrasting emotions of the two skippers, plus bring you the moments that mattered.

Disgraceful scenes as the Argentinian players surround the referee during the Final.

PREVIOUS MEETINGS

Year	Venue	Event	Result
1958	Malmo	WC	West Germany 3, Argentina 1.
1966	Villa Park	WC	West Germany 0, Argentina 0.
1973	Munich	F	West Germany 2, Argentina 3.
1977	Buenos Aires	F	Argentina 1, West Germany 3.
1979	West Berlin	F	West Germany 0, Argentina 1.
1981	Montevideo	GC	Argentina 2, West Germany 1.
1982	Buenos Aires	F	Argentina 1, West Germany 1.
1984	Dusseldorf	F	West Germany 1, Argentina 3.
1986	Mexico City	WCF	Argentina 3, West Germany 2.
1987	Buenos Aires	F	Argentina 1, West Germany 0.
1988	West Berlin	WBT	West Germany 1, Argentina 0.

KEY: F — Friendly; GC — Gold Cup; WBT — West Berlin Tournament; WC — World Cup; WCF — World Cup Final.

● Jorge Burruchaga scored the winning goal in 1984, 1986 and 1987.
● Lothar Matthaus scored the winner in 1988.
● The 1984 match was Franz Beckenbauer's first as West Germany's coach.
● Ruggeri, Burruchaga and Maradona were Argentina's only three survivors from 1986 Final (Note: Olarticoechea, Giusti and Batista also appeared in the 1986 Final but were banned from the 1990 Final).
● Brehme, Berthold, Matthaus and Voeller were the only four survivors from the 1986 defeat.

F THE WORLD!

GERMANY ARE WORTHY WINNERS AS ARGENTINA GO HOME IN DISGRACE

FINAL FACTS

● Monzon is the first player to be sent off in a World Cup Final — Dezotti is the second.

● Franz Beckenbauer is only the second man ever to play for and to manage a World Cup-winning side — the first was Brazil's Mario Zagalo.

● Argentina were the dirtiest team in Italia '90 having three players sent off and 25 booked.

● Twenty eight of the 52 games in the tournament were 0-0 at half-time.

● There were 162 bookings in Italia '90 — that's an average of three a game.

Surrounded by the flashing cameras of the world's Press, Lothar Matthaus raises the World Cup in the night sky of Rome.

WE TOLD YOU SO!

FLASHBACK to our June 9 issue and this is what editor Paul Stratton said in tipping West Germany . . .

"Once again the Germans have gone about their build-up with the quiet efficiency we have come to expect. The likes of Jurgen Klinsmann and Lothar Matthaus ooze class, but it's the steamroller-like teamwork of the Germans that can win the day."

Andreas Brehme tucks away the perfect penalty to win the World Cup for Germany and (above) wheels away in delight.

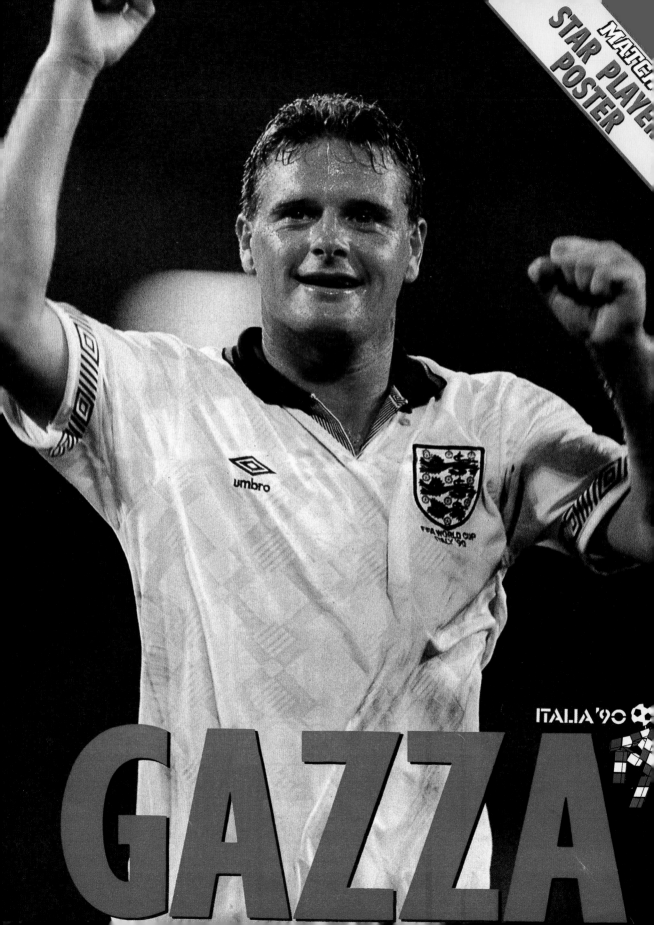

ITALIA '90

GAZZA

BEST OF THE REST!

Horror hair, dodgy beards, vintage adverts and more.

HORROR HAIR!
MEGA MULLETS AND CRAZY CURLS!

3

ERIC GATES SUNDERLAND

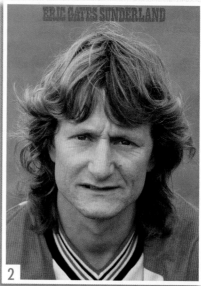

2

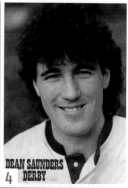

DEAN SAUNDERS DERBY

4

MATCH

5

(1) Walsall's Richard O'Kelly at a photocall before the start of the 1985-86 season, (2) Sunderland's Eric Gates in 1988, (3) Northampton midfielder Richard Hill, (4) Dean Saunders in his Derby days, (5) Sheffield Wednesday right-back Mel Sterland, who spent ten great years with The Owls, (6) West Brom defender Martyn Bennett, (7) Northampton striker Trevor Morley, (8) Lincoln keeper David Felgate, who made nearly 200 appearances for The Imps.

DAVID FELGATE
Lincoln City

6

7

8

9

(9) Alan Brazil's incredible curls before the start of the 1979-80 season, (10) Watford winger Nigel Callaghan, (11) Bolton boss Gary Megson during his days with Sheffield Wednesday, (12) Alan Biley's quality mullet, (13) Robbie Earle in a Port Vale line-up, (14) Tony Coton keeping goal, (15) Man. City's Andy May, (16) Andy Gray playing up front for Wolves, (17) Hibernian's Alistair Brazil.

10

GARY MEGSON
SHEFFIELD WEDNESDAY

11

MATCH

12 **ALAN BILEY Portsmouth**

13

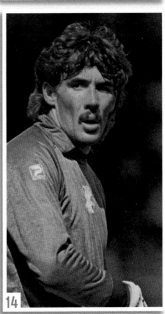

14

15

16

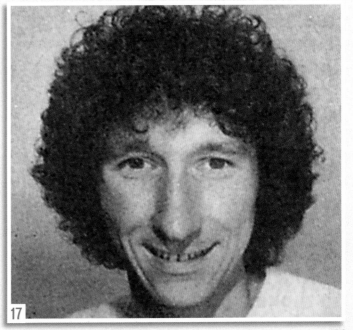

17

BEFORE THEY WERE FAMOUS!
EVEN TV PUNDITS WERE YOUNG ONCE!

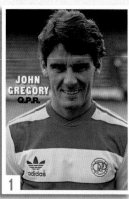

1 JOHN GREGORY Q.P.R.

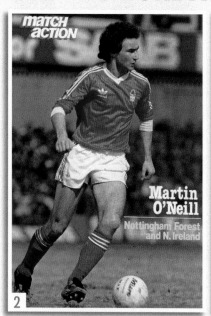

MATCH ACTION

Martin O'Neill
Nottingham Forest and N. Ireland

2

PETERBOROUGH UNITED Season 84/85

3

(1) Former Aston Villa manager John Gregory in his QPR playing days, (2) Martin O'Neill in the red of Nottingham Forest, (3) David Seaman in the back row of a Peterborough line-up at London Road, (4) Special K fan Alan Curbishley, before his days in the West Ham dugout, (5) Steve McClaren smiling for the cameras.

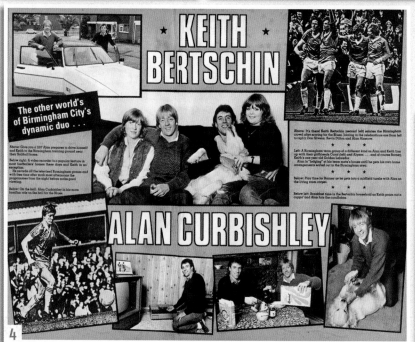

★ KEITH BERTSCHIN ★

The other world's of Birmingham City's dynamic duo . . .

ALAN CURBISHLEY

4

5

(6) A young Diego Maradona before the 1982 World Cup, (7) Harry Redknapp with his Bournemouth team, (8) A curly Bryan Robson at The Hawthorns, (9) Current Aldershot boss Gary Waddock, (10) Reading's Steve Coppell, (11) Wolves boss 'Mike' McCarthy sporting a moustache, (12) Sky Sports pundit Tony Gale, (13) Scotland manager George Burley.

STAR SPOT

Spotlight on Ipswich Town's Scottish international full-back

GEORGE BURLEY

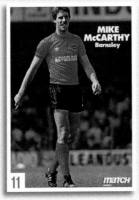

MIKE McCARTHY
Barnsley

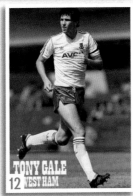

TONY GALE
WEST HAM

FACIAL FUZZ!
DID RAZORS EXIST IN THE '80s?

1

2

THE STARS AND THEIR HEROES

MATCH weekly

Saturday, July 19 1980
25p

PETER WITHE -Villa for the title!

JOE JORDAN -United must improve

3

4

(1) Belgium defender Eric Gerets, *(2)* Stoke's George Berry, *(3)* Aston Villa striker Peter Withe on the cover of MATCH, *(4)* Liverpool No.1 Bruce Grobbelaar, *(5)* Celtic legend Danny McGrain, *(6)* QPR's David Seaman in the days before his ponytail, *(7)* Wolves defender Geoff Palmer during his first spell at Molineux, *(8)* Brian Kilcline before he won the FA Cup with Coventry, *(9)* Brighton's Steve Foster without his trademark headband.

5

6

7

8

9

10

11

MATCH

12

13

14

(10) Alan Devonshire in the middle row of a West Ham photocall, (11) Aston Villa's Dennis Mortimer in 1984, (12) Steve MacKenzie in his West Brom home kit, (13) Frank Lampard Senior hitting one with his right foot during his West Ham days, (14) Brazil legend and doctor of medicine, Socrates, (15) Ipswich and Scotland's goalscoring midfielder John Wark, (16) Luton's Ricky Hill on a MATCH poster in 1982.

15

16

FOOTBALL ADVERTS!
BOOTS, PROGRAMMES, GAMES AND MILK!

1

HOW DO FOOTBALL TEAMS GLIDE OVER THE PITCH?
HOW DO YOU SCORE GOALS WITH A SNOOKER CUE?
HOW DO YOU PLAY SOCCER + SNOOKER TOGETHER?

SNOCCER®
The GREAT new game of the 80's !!

Craftsman built Mahogany tables in 2 sizes
Standard table : 4ft x 32"
De-luxe table : 6ft x 40"

For details of nearest stockists
send S.A.E to
McAllister Sports Games Ltd.
Unit I, Block A, Juno Way
London SE14 5RW

Your favourite teams available!

2

No drink can beat it. Milk is   supreme

Phil Neal scores the winner, so he gets the best seat in the house. But they all get the best drink in the fridge. In fact, milk is so full of natural goodness, it's more than just a drink – it's liquid food. For sheer deliciousness and energy replacement, you can't beat the 'magic potion'.

3

Keep in time with your team
As Ray Clemence does

with a soccer wall clock all four divisions covered plus Scottish
£15.00 plus 95p p&p complete with battery

*Soccer Clocks
The clock with a difference. Your favourite players in correct positions in place of numerals*

WOLVES · MANCHESTER CITY · MANCHESTER UNITED F.C. · CELTIC

LIVERPOOL F.C.

SOCCER CLOCKS, 36 MILL LANE, LIVERPOOL L13 5TF. PLEASE SEND MY SOCCER CLOCK (CLUB NAME)

I ENCLOSE CHEQUE/POSTAL ORDER FOR £15.95 (INC. 95p P&P).

(NAME)

ADDRESS

4

IT'S A WHOLE NEW BALL GAME

CENTAPOST

Gordon Strachan

(1) Mix snooker and soccer, and you get? Snoccer! (2) Phil Neal promotes the benefits of drinking milk for the Milk Marketing Board, (3) Ray Clemence poses with a Soccer Clock, (4) Scotland ace Gordon Strachan with a Centapost, 'probably the most exciting football invention since the ball', (5) Nike's classic Ian Rush advert, (6) Steve Earl Football Programmes, with iconic cartoon seller, (7) Virgin's Anfield Rap, (8) Trevor Francis promotes an early electronic game, (9) Adidas' World Class boots.

MATCH: Best Of The '80s would like to thank the following people for their help in producing this book:

Phil Bagnall for his special insight into photographing MATCH's memorable features from the past 28 years. Mel Bagnall for revealing the illustrator behind the Harry Cannon cartoon strip. Graham Lampard and his staff at Craftsman Binders in Northampton for unbinding 11 seasons worth of MATCH magazines. Sue Battey at Newcastle United Football Club for working with us on Kevin Keegan's book foreword. Andreas Nilsson at the Swedish FA for confirming that Kevin Keegan is battling Sweden's Conny Torstensson on the first MATCH cover. Lara Thorns & Jim Brown at Coventry City Football Club for confirming that the team played in the infamous brown kit between 1978-81. Martin Ellis at PA Photos for allowing us to use classic 1980s football pictures from their archives. Billy Robertson at Action Images for allowing us to reproduce their football photos that appeared in MATCH. Rob Hughes at Adidas, Paul Smith at Freud PR, Steve Earl at Steve Earl Football Programmes, Jessie Yeomans at The Dairy Council, Gemma Bolton at Hasbro, Anne Olesen at Tomy and Frances Harding at EMI Group Limited for allowing us to reproduce their adverts. Billys Vinyl Emporium for supplying us with two MATCH 'Mastermind Of Soccer' 7" quiz records. Susan Voss for helping us with our copyright and legal issues.

MATCH: Best Of The '80s is dedicated to Harry Street and Ben Unwin – we hope you enjoy your first football book, kids.